FREDERICK CATHERWOOD
ARCH^{t.}

'The Stream of Time,' wrote Lord Verulam, thinking perhaps of his own decline and fall, 'lets every substance sink and carries down with it only the froth and the foam.' Whether or not Francis Bacon was thinking of himself, he does not say, yet he might well have written it for his latter-day countryman, Frederick Catherwood; it could well have been his epitaph.

This, then, is the impersonal personal history of Frederick Catherwood, who, though sunk in the 'Stream of Time,' has now emerged from the obscurity that has veiled him for a century as one of the greatest of archaeological explorers. An explorer of two worlds, East and West, Catherwood was a trained architect who, in the earliest days of archaeological science, explored the buried civilizations of Rome, of Greece, of Egypt, the burned-out civilizations of Transjordania, the cultures that rimmed the Mediterranean, and the buried cities of the Maya in Yucatán.

Familiar with the great and near great of his time, known personally to all its architects and artists, a friend of John Keats and Joseph Severn, an acquaintance of Shelley, Byron, Trelawney, and the other members of the Society of Englishmen in Rome, Frederick Catherwood has not endured in their histories even as a footnote. In American history, he who enlivened the New York scene in the 'Age of Jackson' with his panoramas, his buildings, and his Central American explorations, figures only as a shadowy, unrealized, figure.

This then, is an attempt to raise Frederick Catherwood out of the alluvium of the 'Stream of Time,' to cover him with flesh, and give him life.

I first discovered 'Mr. Catherwood,' as thousands had before me, while reading the delectable pages of Stephens' *Incidents of Travel in Yucatán*. Later when writing a life of John Lloyd Stephens,* I came into further contact with the enigmatical 'Mr. Catherwood.' Since as the biographer of one it became incumbent upon me to know something of the other, I began a search for something of Catherwood's *curriculum vitae;* I haunted the encyclopedias, the biographical dictionaries, and the lexicons, and I was rewarded with nothing. Then, remembering that Catherwood had for ten years been associated with archaeological explorations in Rome, Greece, and Egypt, I turned to the publications and museums that specialized in Mediterranean cultures. Once again, nothing. Everywhere the results of inquiry were negative. It was as if some spiteful poltergeist had followed in Catherwood's wake, destroying every page of his life's testimony. The Library of Congress, whose bibliographical records are almost exhaustive, had only Catherwood's name and the titles of his meager bibliography on their reference cards. Nor had the British Museum more. The institutions of which he had been a member, the Royal Institute of British Architects, the Royal Astronomical Society, possessed only the scantiest material.

At this moment of failure I was prepared to allow my unwilling subject to remain in his limbo. Yet, there was a challenge here. It seemed hardly possible that a man, who had made such great contributions to archaeology and architectural history, not alone in the New World but in the Old World as well, should not have left somewhere an account of the essential details of his wander-

---

* *Maya Explorer, John Lloyd Stephens and the Lost Cities of Central America and Yucatán*, University of Oklahoma Press, Norman, Okla., 1947.

ings. Somewhere proved to be everywhere. In response to my letters of inquiry there came from Egypt, Syria, Denmark, England, British Guiana, Scotland—and geographically everywhere in America—fragments of his life. Slowly, like Dr. Faustus's *homumculus*, Catherwood took on flesh, personality, and movement, and finally evolved as he now appears herein, albeit shadowy and indistinct.

This restoration of Frederick Catherwood has been possible only through the aid of many individuals and institutions; Miss Bartlett Cowdrey of New York, an authority on nineteenth-century art, turned over to me the scattered notes she had collected on Catherwood, and helped in other ways too many to detail. The entire staff of the New-York Historical Society gave me unstinted assistance and the use of their Catherwood collection; Miss Etheldred Abbot, Librarian of the Ryerson and Burnham Libraries in Chicago, brought to my attention the article on Catherwood in the *Dictionary of Architecture*; Mr. J. Christian Bay, of John Crear Library, supplied me the bibliography of Panoramas; Dr. Lawrence C. Wroth implemented my 'hunch' by finding the John Russell Bartlett *Journal* and his correspondence with Frederick Catherwood in the collections of the John Carter Brown Library; the staff of the Massachusetts Historical Society found the Prescott-Catherwood correspondence; Miss Mabel R. Gillis, State Librarian of California, found the newspaper material relating to Catherwood's railroad-building activities in California; and Miss Elizabeth Riefstahl, Librarian of the Wilbour Library, Brooklyn Museum, discovered some of the important details touching on Catherwood's Egyptian explorations. These are only a few who helped me, but there are others: Mrs. Frederic G. Hoppin of New York, who allowed me to photograph and use her original Catherwood water color 'Mt. Etna from the Ruins of Tauramina'; Dr. George G.

Heye, who permitted me to reproduce Catherwood's original sepia of the ruins of Uxmal; and finally Mrs. Sarah C. W. Hoppin of Oyster Bay, Long Island, who aided me in various way, the least of which was the discovery of many original Catherwoods.

From British Guiana I had the aid of Mr. Vincent Roth, in charge of that Colony's Museums, who ferreted out Catherwood's original reports on the Demerera Railroad and had them typed for me; and from Copenhagen, Dr. Paul Bergsoe, found for me the originals of Catherwood's drawings of Newport Tower.

In England I had the aid and enthusiastic assistance of many generous people, who despite their bleak times and buried records, assisted me in the re-creation of Frederick Catherwood: from His Majesty King George VI an unpublished letter from Humboldt to Prince Albert in which Catherwood was the subject; from Mr. Edward Carter, former Librarian of the Royal Institute of British Architects (now with UNESCO), many letters, each containing details of importance; from the British Museum (Department of Manuscripts), aid in the selection and photography of documents relating to Frederick Catherwood in the Egyptological collections of Robert Hay; from the Victoria and Albert Museum (South Kensington), photographs of the Egyptian sketches of Catherwood; from Keats' Memorial House, Hampstead, permission to copy and use the Keats-Severn correspondence that relates to Catherwood; from Lady Mary Unwin, the great-granddaughter of one of the Severns, additional material on Catherwood. Miss Rosalind Moss of the Ashmolean Museum, Oxford, and Mr. Percy E. Newberry gave me considerable aid on Catherwood's Egyptian explorations. Finally, I wish to express my deep gratitude to Mr. C. M. Jackson, Borough Librarian of Shoreditch, for photographing Catherwood's ancestral home, still standing at Charles Square, Hoxton, and discovering, after much work, the names of his parents. And to close this long list, my sincere thanks to Miss Sylvia

England, my 'eyes and ears,' my research assistant in London, and to Professor Talbot Hamlin, architectural historian of Columbia University, for a critical reading of the manuscript.

To all who have so generously aided me in breathing life back into Frederick Catherwood, my deepest gratitude.

V. W. v.H.

Hickory Hill
Westport, Conn.
August, 1949

Plates

List of Illustrations

It was in Guatemala, while trying to do a little sketching among the almost unbelievably picturesque ruins of Antigua, that I first became interested in Frederick Catherwood. With his drawings of Mayan steles and temples — or rather with the woodcuts, which other hands than his had made, none too competently, after those drawings — I was, of course, already familiar. But to the man who was responsible for those amazingly accurate and vivid works of documentary art, I had previously given no thought. My concern with Catherwood as a person was aroused by the insects. To the would-be landscape painter, even in salubrious Antigua, these are a very severe trial. I bore with them for a couple of hours, then packed up my paints, discomfited and full of a new admiration for the man who had made the illustrations to Stephens's *Incidents of Travel.* From dawn till dusk, day after day and for weeks at a stretch, this martyr to archaeology had exposed himself to all the winged and crawling malice of tropical nature. Ticks, ants, wasps, flies, mosquitoes; they had bitten him, stung him, drunk his blood, infected him with malaria. But the man had grimly gone on drawing. Itching, swollen, burning or shuddering with fever, he had filled whole portfolios with the measured plans and elevations of temples, with studies of Mayan sculpture so scientifically accurate that modern experts in pre-Columbian history can spell out the date of a stele from Catherwood's representations of its, to him, incomprehensible hieroglyphs.

This gifted artist, this conscientiously precise and careful observer, this indomitable Prometheus, self-chained to his camp-stool, while the mosquitoes brought him again and again to the very gates of death — who was he? Returning from Central America to libraries and books of reference, I tried to find out — but with absolutely no success. Catherwood remained merely a name and nothing more. But now Mr. Victor von Hagen, an explorer of jungles who is also an explorer of explorers, has undertaken the task of restoring to this name a history and a personality. Thanks to his labors we now know where Catherwood was born, how he was educated, to what temples, pyramids, mosques, and acropolises his passion for archaeology took him. And we know too that Catherwood was dogged throughout his whole career as an archaeologist and artist by a bad luck, so perfectly adapted to thwart his ambitions, so exquisitely designed to frustrate all his best efforts, as to seem the conscious working of a kind of negative Providence. Most of his innumerable studies of Egyptian ruins remained unpublished, and the same fate was reserved for his elaborate architectural drawings — the first ever made — of the Mosque of Omar at Jerusalem. Later, when he began to make money in New York, his crowd-drawing panorama of the Holy City was destroyed by fire, and along with the circular building and his enormous painting, hundreds of original drawings brought back from Central America were also destroyed. After that, it is not surprising to learn, Catherwood abandoned the unequal struggle with a Destiny, which evidently had no intention of allowing him to be a successful artist and archaeologist. He packed up, parked a wife and perhaps a child or two, and vanished.

> *What's become of Waring,*
> *Since he gave us all the slip?*

Alas, it was not in Vishnu-land that this precursor of Browning's hero was to be found; it was not over the Kremlin's pavement that he 'stepped with five other generals, who simultaneously take snuff'; it was not even to the romantic obscurity of a Triestine bum-boat that he had retired. Poor Catherwood had disappeared into British Guiana, where, no longer calling himself an architect or painter or archaeologist, but a civil engineer, he was building the first railway to be laid down on the soil of South America. Or, to be more precise, he was trying to build it. Good artists, as Rimbaud was to demonstrate a generation later, are rarely good businessmen or administrators. Besides, this particular project turned out to be unexpectedly difficult. The terrain was marshy; the Negro laborers would not labor; the white planters were unsympathetic; the climate and the insects were, if possible, worse than those of Yucatán and Guatemala. Catherwood's negative Providence was still busily at work upon him. After a year or two he threw up the sponge and retired, by way of Panama, to newly booming California. Here, it seems, he might at long last have prospered. But this was something which his Destiny could obviously not permit. It put into his head the idea of paying a visit to England and, on the return voyage, arranged a collision on the high seas, which sent the one-time artist and archaeologist, along with many other passengers, to the bottom of the Atlantic.

Thus ended Frederick Catherwood, plunging irretrievably and for ever into that ocean of oblivion, from which, even in life, he had hardly succeeded in emerging. For not only had he failed to receive that public recognition to which his talents entitled him; he seems also, in some sort, to have missed even private recognition. He was the friend and collaborator of painters and draftsmen; yet no likeness of him was ever made — or, at any rate, none is now extant. He worked for many months with a vivid and copious writer, and he had met, in the course of his wandering life, many journalists in search of copy and many archaeologists who shared his special interests; and yet none of them has left us an account of his personality or of the details of his private life. In spite of Mr. von Hagen's researches, the man whose strange and in many ways tragic career he has now reconstructed remains profoundly mysterious. We know what he did; but we still have very little idea what he was like, or how he thought or felt.

Professionally speaking, Catherwood belongs to a species — the artist-archaeologist — which is all but extinct. What the rifle did to *Bos bison,* the camera has done to that breed of which Piranesi was the most celebrated specimen and Catherwood his not unworthy successor. In the fiftieth of a second a man with a Leica can do what Catherwood could accomplish only at the cost of long, agonizing days among the insects, followed by months or years of intermittent fever. Or, to be more accurate, the man with the Leica can do *some* of the things that Catherwood and Piranesi did, and do them better than even the most masterly and con- scientious of draftsmen. But when we pass from the precise repro- duction of architectural and sculptural details to the rendering of great monuments in their totality, as their creators meant them to be seen and as the mind behind the spectator's eyes actually per- ceives them, the advantage is not always with the photographer. The camera is unable, while it does its recording, to turn its head or lift his eyes. Except from a great distance, it cannot take in the whole of a large monument, while at close range it sees receding lines and surfaces in a perspective that, by human standards, always seems exaggerated. No photograph of the Colosseum or the aque- ducts of the Campagna, of Castel Sant' Angelo or the Roman basilicas can compare (leaving out of account all questions of intrinsic beauty) even in mere truthfulness with the etchings of Piranesi. For Piranesi renders not only the details but also the impression made by the monuments as artistic wholes. It is only by taking many partial views that the photographer is able to make up for his instrument's inability to render the full effect of an architectural totality. And of course this endless capacity for partial views does in fact make the camera more useful to the archaeologist than the pencil, even though, given a sufficiency of time, talent, and resistance to insects, he can do things with the pencil which are beyond the scope of his optical machine. But time is limited, talent is very rare, and mosquitoes distressingly abundant. Hence the extinction of the proud race of artist-archae-ologists. Catherwood and his kind have now gone the way of the engravers on steel and copper, of the mezzotinters, the wood-block makers, and those wonderful cartoonist-lithographers and jour-nalist-draftsmen, of whom Daumier and Constantin Guys were the greatest. Illustrated papers now rely on snapshots and process blocks, and pictures are reproduced by collotype or photogravure. The second-rate artists, who were once so usefully employed in making intrinsically beautiful reproductions of the works of their betters, are now at liberty to devote the whole of their attention to 'creative work.' In other words, they are now free to spend all their time producing the rubbish, of which alone, as original artists, they are capable.

ALDOUS HUXLEY

FREDERICK CATHERWOOD

ARCH^{t.}

Chapter One

HOXTON

Frederick Catherwood was born, in the last year of the eighteenth century, in London's Hoxton Parish. Of the circumstances of his birth, we know scarcely more. It was a period of candlelight, powdered periwigs, and ten-syllabled couplets. And of wits. Wits, satirizing the youthful Prime Minister, William Pitt:

> A sight to make surrounding nations stare,
> A kingdom trusted to a schoolboy's care.

The Catherwoods, to give something, no matter how rudimentary, of their genealogy, were a Scotch-Irish family who had settled since the previous century in the environs of London. The name Catherwood, a rather uncommon one, originally derived from the river Calder, which flows near Edinburgh, was once 'Calderwood,' until the alchemy of usage turned it into 'Ca-a-erwood,' and thence into its present form. There is no record of any Catherwood before Frederick having connection with the arts, unless one include the 'Mr. Catherwood a goldsmith in Ireland' mentioned in 1773, in *Archaeologia*.[1] Yet if the Catherwoods did not bear the stamp of the aristocracy, neither did they suffer the opprobrium of being lower middle class; they were undoubtedly people of substance. John Catherwood, who flourished *circa* 1715, when medical doctors were half-alchemists, half barber-surgeons, wrote a learned treatise on apoplexy, *Disputatie de apoplexia*, and supplemented it with one in English, *A New*

3

Method of Curing the Apoplexy; that is all we know of the first 'historical' Catherwood. He is followed in the same century by another named John James Catherwood, whose interest seemingly turned toward economics, as evidenced by a publication, *An Account of the Quantities of Corn and Grain from and Imported into England and Scotland.*[2] This gentleman was Frederick's uncle, who resided at 21, Charles Square, Hoxton. Immediately next door at Number 20 was the residence of the other 'Catherwoods,' they were Nathaniel and Elizabeth Catherwood, the parents of Frederick Catherwood. He was born in that house 27 February 1799.

North of the Thames, eight miles beyond the Old Lady of Threadneedle Street, where Bishopsgate Street becomes Hackney Road, lies the metropolitan Borough of Shoreditch. Once a village on the old Roman Road, Shoreditch is composed of two districts, one of which (called 'Hochestone' in the *Domesday Book*) is the hamlet of Hoxton. In ancient times a village, Hoxton was then a prebend of St. Paul's Cathedral, an extraparochial district, 'where the inhabitants maintained their own peer, married and buried where they pleased.'[3]

Hoxton always had an air about it, although Sir Walter Besant claimed it was the effluvia of sewers,[4] for the etymology of Shoreditch did not originate, as some claimed, from Jane Shore, the mistress of Edward IV, but had evolved from 'sewer ditch,' since the *cloacal fossa* of London Town emptied somewhere in the vicinity of its Hoxton fields. Yet the Hoxton air had something more than the miasma of London's sewers; Will Shakespeare was supposed to have acted at the theater called the Curtain, in Shoreditch;[5] *Romeo and Juliet,* it is believed, had its première there. And there Ben Jonson fought a duel with an actor, arising out of an argument over the scanning of some verse; his disparager he dispatched with a thrust in tierce, sending this Gabriel Spender, his entrails all perforated, to the Shoreditch graveyard to rest beside Will Somers, sometime court jester to Henry VIII. And there were other worthies once resident in Hoxton—Edmund Halley, Astronomer Royal, had been born there, as had John Newton,[6] the famous incumbent of St. Mary's Woolnoths and the friend of William Cowper.* Keats' three brothers were baptized at St. Leonard's, Shoreditch; the author of *Frankenstein* lived in Essex Street in Hoxton before she joined her lover Percy Shelley in Italy—and Kate Greenaway, who gave us the Age of Innocence unchilled and unhurt was also a Hoxtonion. And so Hoxton did have a literary air. It also possessed a mild atmosphere of lunacy.

The 'mad World of Hoxton' referred scarcely to the merry goings-on at the Pimlico Ale-House, but to Balmes House, the magnificent seventeenth-century manor, which had been converted into an insane asylum. It was here, in fact, that the Lambs, Mary and Charles, had intermittent residence after Mary Lamb, in 1796, killed her mother with a carving knife. The Balmes House— hence the word balmy—had set the insane precedent; soon other mental institutions crowded into once-fashionable Hoxton, so many that even John Hollingshead remembered in his autobiography that his bedroom overlooked a private mad-house.[7] But by the beginning of the nineteenth century Hoxton had already attracted 'smaller industries and lesser ingenuities,' haberdashers, furniture makers, and engravers, and its open fields became crowded with bleak houses of villeins in breed and tenure; Hoxton was on its way to become, as Sir Walter Besant later called it, 'The Queen of Unloveliness.'

Charles Square, Hoxton, where the Catherwoods lived, had escaped the general leveling. It was a small, delightful square surrounded by houses built about 1770—and, as the *Shoreditch Observer* recorded, 'occupied by a highly respectable class of persons.'

---

* The suppressed preface of John Newton to Cowper's *Poems* is dated '1782, Charles Sq.'

Two of these houses facing Charles Square, houses with classical doors and iron grills, were the Catherwood's.[8]

While war in Europe raged, Frederick Catherwood sought an education. For those not automatically established by family position, an education or a place in the world was not easily acquired; education for the sons of people of meager circumstances was almost unheard of. Catherwood attended one of those home-spun day schools—the Haberdashers school (otherwise Aske's) near to Charles Square, which had originated in the will of Robert Aske for The Worshipful Company of Haberdashers for the education of Freemen's sons.[9] In the early nineteenth century its facilities were extended to the children of Hoxton. There, presumably, Catherwood remained to the Eighth Form studying Accidence and Grammar, and becoming, at least to the satisfaction of the awarded certificates, 'a perfect grammarian, a good Orator and Poet, well instructed in Latin, Greek and Hebrew.' Yet it must have been a thorough education, for Catherwood became later an excellent linguist, able to speak Arabic, Greek, and Italian, and read, if not write, Hebrew; he had enough 'Mathematicks' to prepare him for his profession of architect.

Still it was outside his classes that his life interest developed: he became passionately interested in architecture.

Catherwood wandered with his friend Joseph Severn through the labyrinths of London's alleys and lanes, where new buildings were rising to ornament England's Augustan Age. Severn, Hoxton-born and four years the senior of Catherwood, who would enter literary history as the *fidus Achates* of John Keats, was already apprenticed to William Bond, the engraver, of Newman Street, Hoxton.[10] Perhaps Severn's act gave Catherwood the needed inspiration, for when he reached sixteen and left school he was brought to Michael Meredith, the architect, who lived on Bishopsgate Road. In 1815 Catherwood signed articles of apprenticeship; he was to remain with Meredith for five years, from 1815 until 1820.

6

Chapter Two

THE ROMANTIC AGONY

Frederick Catherwood, accompanying his master, Michael Meredith, Arch^t., made a topographical tour of England. It was the day of the beautifully illustrated architectural book made popular by John Britton, and Meredith followed this trend, dragging with him his apprentice. Nothing much is known of Michael Meredith except for his exhibition record at the Royal Academy,[1] the titles of which suggest that he was deeply enmeshed in the 'romantic agony,' an inheritance undoubtedly from his father, George Meredith, the eighteenth-century architect. Under Meredith, Catherwood learned his craft. He was taught the mechanics of drawing, isometrical projection, perspective, and skiography, and under Meredith's tutorship he became an excellent performer with T-square and compass. Between the intervals of work Catherwood cleaned the palettes, sketched in the rough work of his master, and did the thousand and one disagreeable tasks of an apprentice. Thus for five years he lived on a pittance and learned his profession.

Architecture, the most rational and physical of the arts, was, in the moment of Catherwood's apprenticeship, torn by the battle of styles, two distinct traditions, a dual movement as it were— the Classic and the Romantic, each contending for public attention. These architectural styles, violently in opposition, were reflected in the public buildings erected in that period. The Houses of Parliament were a triumph of the Romantic, with their

7

long straggling lines, disproportionate towers, and monotonous detail. The Bank of England, on the contrary, marked the momentary ascendency of the Classical school.

The Gothicists—couching their ideas in turgid Byronic language—created in architecture the cult of the picturesque. In this they were in tune with the times. It was the age of swooning ladies, of gentle melancholy—of world-weariness, the kind of *Weltschmerz* found in *The Sorrows of Young Werther*. The Romantic artists were also busy with the picturesque, their pictures, studded with ruins, turbulent cataracts, forests of thick-trunked trees, gloomy, fractured walls, had the 'tempestuous loveliness of terror' running through the entire range of their work. In art young Catherwood found a whole cult dedicated to the picturesque; there were Thomas Girtin, Turner's feared rival, Michael 'Angelo' Rooker, Samuel Prout (a master of dilapidation, who later used many of Catherwood's sketches for some effective canvases), David Roberts, James Holland, and W. J. Müller. And above them all was the high priest of the Romanticists, John Martin, whose gigantic canvases, Belshazzar's Feast and Overwhelming of Sodom, were developed in the intricate overtones of the Romantic vocabulary.[2] Frederick Catherwood could not escape the influence of the picturesque or of the Classical 'approach'; but in him and his art both were syncretized.

There were, of course, limitations to his apprenticeship with Michael Meredith. Catherwood found after five years that he had gone as far as he could with this master. In 1820, he received back his apprentice-indentures and immediately began to work on his first exhibition piece.

It was Joseph Severn, his boyhood friend from Hoxton, who urged him to continue his studies. Severn, who had risen to comparatively dizzy heights since they had last met, had won, the year before, the Gold Medal of the Royal Academy for his heroic-sized, canvas, 'The Cave of Despair,' a theme taken from Edmund

Spenser. Severn had not changed greatly since their Hoxton days. He had the same slight figure, the same dreamy eyes, the weak mouth and chin that suggested the sentimentalist; but his manner, as always, was light, easy, and gay. With medal, reputation, and a scholarship, Joseph Severn was not to be taken lightly; he suggested further study at the Academy to Catherwood, who immediately enrolled. A new life suddenly opened to Catherwood, for his friend Severn had already been admitted into Leigh Hunt's circle and he was, by 1820, an acquaintance if not an intimate friend of John Keats. Although there is no precise record of it, Catherwood probably became through Severn a member of this 'Keats Circle.' [3] It is obvious from the Catherwood-Severn correspondence that he met young Keats at his College Street lodgings when the young poet was in the first stages of phthisis; Catherwood little dreamed then how the fatal illness of a young poet would be bound up with his own destiny.

Curiously enough, no one has ever described Catherwood, and his own self-portrait picture is but a luminous blur. Although he was known personally to almost every important artist or architect of his time and to many of the artists studying in Rome and to the regiment of artist-explorers (his colleagues) who toured Egypt (and later a personal friend of most of the National Academicians in New York City), no one, for unfathomable reasons, ever drew or painted the reticent 'Mr. Catherwood'—at least there is no known record of any portrait of him. Even among the hundred drawings of William Brockedon [4]—now in the British Museum—containing pencilings of almost every one of Catherwood's contemporaries, there is none of him. In a rare autobiographical gesture Catherwood made a self-portrait of himself and his friend Joseph Bonomi for a 'Panorama of Jerusalem,' but this has been destroyed. There remains only his other self-portrait, in miniature and unclear, standing before one of the ruins of the Mayan site of Tulum.[5] He is here pictured as a mature man of forty-two; he

9

drew himself as he undoubtedly was—as ruggedly constructed as a Dorchester fishing-boat. Here he is pictured light-haired and blue-eyed. One can make out no more. Nor is there a word description of Catherwood; he is only referred to, even by his most intimate friends, as 'Mr. Catherwood.' John Lloyd Stephens, who knew him intimately for fifteen years, and traveled with him through strife-torn Central America, enduring with him imprisonment, disease, and incredible hardships, speaks of him only as 'Mr. Catherwood.'

Catherwood himself, is responsible for the meagerness of his personal history; there was some fundamental disequilibrium in his psyche. He was modest to a fault; he pushed the classic English virtues—dignity, serenity, reticence—to such a point that he diminished his own personality. Formal and restrained, he exhibited early symptoms of melancholia, often lapsing—for reasons never wholly clear—into periods of morose silence. But he had enthusiasm, despite his reserved and retiring manner, and this was to sustain him while, in the narrow corners of some lost world, he delineated the remains of forgotten civilizations. What his reaction to the 'Keats Circle' was we shall never know. In all this exalted discourse he must have felt ill at ease, still he could not but have been grateful to Joseph Severn for his inclusion in the sparkling circle.

In 1820, under Joseph Severn's guidance, Catherwood began to attend the free art classes of the Royal Academy, in London. Held at Somerset House, the school was opened, *sine pecunia*, to qualified pupils. Although it was closed between March and August, it was still the only one in London, unless one excepts the atelier of Henry Sass in Bloomsbury.

Catherwood, having passed the examinations, attended its classes. There he found Henry Fuseli, the Swiss-born fantasist, giving classes in drawing, explaining his ideas in an amusing Katzenjammer dialect; the great J. M. W. Turner explained perspective, and Sir John Soane gave the lectures on architecture.

Soane's lectures, although given in his small colorless voice, were the popular feature of the Royal Academy. In attendance were many young architectural students with whom Catherwood would make archaeological history—T. J. Donaldson, Henry Parke, Francis Arundale, Joseph John Scoles, and Joseph Bonomi. Soane, 'the most original British Architect since Vanbrugh,' [6] was a twinkle-eyed enthusiastic little man, the son of a bricklayer, and had in his youth been articled out to the architect George Dance. He studied at the Royal Academy and, in the year that the American colonies were declaring themselves independent, won the society's Gold Medal for 'A Triumphal Bridge.' He traveled in Italy and Greece, studying the classical forms, and in Rome he 'discovered' Piranesi. One of the pioneers of the Greek Revival, (although his classicism was always subservient to his rationalism) Sir John Soane was also a practicing architect; he designed the Bank of England, the Loggie to the Governor's Court, and the famous Tyringham House. At the age of 53 he began his lectures at the Royal Academy.

Frederick Catherwood became saturated with Soane's 'first principals.' He learned from him of domes, blocking courses, arches, pediments, pedestals; and more, for—'the student,' Soane said, 'must also draw the human figure with correctness and have a competent knowledge of Painting and Sculpture. . . He must read much and reflect more. He must live in the bosom of his Profession; for Architecture is too coy a Mistress to be won without constant attention.' [7]

Soane began his lecture with the ancients. Since he could quote no one else, he quoted Pliny on the Egyptian pyramids; he entered into Greek architecture, discussed all the 'Orders'; and made frequent reference to Vitruvius. By the fourth lecture, Soane had approached 'Theory and Practice' ending with: 'Then

Chapter Three

THE ARCHAEOLOGICAL TOUR

1

In response to the fervent entreaties of Severn, morose and melancholy after Keats' death, Frederick Catherwood went to Rome. And this curiously enough is recorded. Joseph Severn, writing to his sister Maria [1] on 15 September 1821, told of this arrival at his rooms at 43 via di San Isidoro in Rome. . .

. . . Mr. Catherwood arrived here last night in perfect health and safety after a most favourable journey. I found him sitting in my Study with the same look and manner that I recollect in London— for he is the first Friend I have met here whom I knew there—his face and voice carried me to my dear home—and I was overjoyed to find you all happy. . . From your intimation I had long expected him —but I have this great pleasure of meeting him before I could calculate—it is a great pleasure and will be also a mutual improvement. We have this Mor^g. seen St. Peters—and the Vatican—with which he is quite delighted or I should say astonished—I have introduced him to many brother Artists here—Englishmen—there are three architects among them [T. J. Donaldson, Joseph Bonomi and J. J. Scoles]— whom he will begin to study with. It was very fortunate you sent me notice [of Catherwood's coming] for I have since taken a set of Rooms of a Russian Artist (as he is soon going away) at a most reasonable rate—and with every possible convenience for us two—There are 2 Studys 2 sitting rooms 2 Bed rooms—and a view all over Rome—with furniture etc—We are to pay no more than £1. 12 per month for the whole. We consider this a most lucky hit—and it comes from your giving me notice—therefore we both most humbly thank you for saving us some 3 £ per month or more—for Lodgings will be enormously dear and are now from the numbers of English coming. Mr. Catherwood found me in good health and spirits—and in the midst of many delightful Studies and speculations &c with many friends—The air in Rome is not unhealthy this season—so that I have remained here at the present time the weather and air is most delicious. Mr. C[atherwood] found this in the Morᵍˢ. walk—he seems most gratified with what we tell of Rome and living in it. I think he has done wisely in coming whilst he is young—he will lay a foundation here that may direct nobly all through Life. . . Mr. Catherwood begs you to show my letter at Charles Square [the residence of the Catherwoods] and prays them to excuse him writing this Post—his head is so full of Rome and Sleep and he is so tired—that he humbly hopes to be permitted to go to bed—He desires me to present his love and remembrance to all that is dear to him—his Home—he says he can never stay here more than a year without seeing them—Like wise make my respects and thanks for permitting him to join me here in Rome—it will be my pleasure to serve him every way possible.

Catherwood was welcomed into the Society of Englishmen, 'all good fellows—20 in number—Painters, Sculptors & Architects,' wrote Joseph Severn.[2] And it was in that group he began his study of classical architecture. The group was exceedingly lively and enthusiastic. One of the four architects, Thomas Leverton Donaldson, the founder-to-be of the Royal Institute of British Architects and a lifelong friend of Catherwood, had been born in Bloomsbury Square in 1795, had studied at the Royal Academy, and had been awarded its Silver Medal. Thereafter, in pursuit of the *antique*, he left for Rome. One of his architectural publications, that on classical doorways,* became in effect the handbook for American architects during the Greek Revival. Having resided abroad since 1819, and having had the longest residence in Italy, Donaldson acted as architectural cicerone to the others—Catherwood, Henry Parke, Joseph Scoles, and Joseph Bonomi.

---

* *A Collection of the Most Approved Examples of Doorways from Ancient Examples in Greece and Italy* (London 1833).

Henry Parke, the oldest of the group, had been the favorite pupil of Sir John Soane and had traveled with him to France. Born in Owen Square in 1792, he had at first studied for the bar, but his passion was architecture and he enrolled at the Royal Academy, where he was discovered by Soane. In Italy he had known Shelley and had been one of the mourners of John Keats, whose funeral he attended. He was to spend four years with Catherwood wandering over the magical lands of the Mediterranean. On his death in 1835 he bequeathed five hundred drawings to the Royal Institute of British Architects.[3]

The other two architects of the Society of Englishmen, Scoles and Bonomi, arrived in Rome a few months after Frederick Catherwood. Scoles, the least remembered of them, had also studied the *antique* in the Royal Academy after he had finished his apprenticeship to Joseph Ireland, architect. Born into the Catholic Church in 1798, Scoles is remembered now, if he is at all, as one of those present at Shelley's funeral; also for his great fiasco, the collapse of the suspension bridge, which he built in 1845, over the river Bure at Great Yarmouth. Scoles was a constant companion of Catherwood in the Mediterranean, and long after he married and fathered four sons and eight daughters, he remained in touch with him. It is to Joseph John Scoles that we owe the only published biographical material—tantalizing though it is—on Catherwood.[4]

Joseph Bonomi, the famous curator of Sir John Soane's Museum at Lincoln Inn Field, is by far the best remembered of all these members of the Society of Englishmen. As the illustrator of Sir John Gardner Wilkinson's works on Egyptian archaeology, Bonomi's name is most enduringly linked to Egypt. He was a gay small man and remembered in that circle of temperamental and perverse artists for his easy good nature. The son of Bonomi, the elder, (the Italian architect who had been brought from Rome on the invitation of the Brothers Adam), Joseph Bonomi was

16

born in 1796 and inherited his father's talents. He attended the Royal Academy and became one of its silver medalists. In company with Scoles he went to Rome. Later, he and Bonomi and Catherwood were included as architectural artists on the famous Egyptian expeditions of Robert Hay.

Rome, in 1822, was filled with English aristocracy who were living elegantly in the villas of impecunious Roman nobles. There, in that properly regal setting, the great milords made obeisance to the Muses. At that time, everyone of consequence, it seemed, was in Rome: Lord Colchester, Speaker of the House, was an art patron in the grand manner; Elizabeth, Duchess of Devonshire was making archaeological excavations in the Forum; and Sir William Drummond, Lord Seymour, the Hon. Henry Fox of the tart-tongued *Diary,* and a host of others who were extending the Grand Tour by living in the dilettante society of the Italian courts. A gentleman then could never be excused from his duty to the Muses, and a seemingly endless succession of artists, sculptors, architects, and writers were working in Rome under the munificence of the aristocracy, a society 'which was literary, athletic, dissipated and political' and, it might be added, slightly confused by the presence of those two egregious bluestockings, the Ladies Westmoreland and Blessington.

Catherwood soon found himself part of this dazzling group to which Joseph Severn had provided the key; he soon was admitted to the *conversazioni* of Roman society and found himself a guest at many Lucculan-like dinners, surrounded by the members of European and English aristocracy, poets, artists, fops, 'company numerous but very ill-sorted.' As Henry Fox complains,[5] 'people of all descriptions without any connection or acquaintance with each other . . . gathered together and huddled up at the dinner table . . . ,' combinations that included Lady Blessington, Elizabeth, the Duchess of Devonshire, Louis Bonaparte and his empty, foolish brother Jerôme, Canova, Thorwaldsen, Duc de Laval, the ephebic Count D'Orsay, Gibson, Severn, Eastlake, Lady Westmoreland, Manuel de Godoy, the fallen Spanish prime minister, Sir William Drummond, and Edward Cheney. Such company was heady wine for young Catherwood, born of modest circumstances and of a family who prided themselves on their liberal ideas.

A few months after his arrival Catherwood became acquainted with the nobility. Lady Westmoreland already had Joseph Severn under siege and he, wishing to lessen the pressure, brought his friend, Catherwood, into the engagement. Lady Westmoreland—Jane to her intimates—the dazzling wife of the sixteenth Earl of Westmoreland, had suddenly become enamored of Egypt. For, at that moment Giovanni Belzoni, the circus-performer turned archaeologist, was battering open one of the pyramids, and a wave of Egyptianism swept over the land. Lady Westmoreland suggested an expedition up the Nile with Joseph Severn attached to her party as artist; Milady had, possibly, more in mind than the mere drawing of pyramids. Severn, who was then finishing his picture 'The Death of Alcibiades' as part of Royal Academy scholarship, declined the offer. But he suggested the name of another young artist named Catherwood, whom he had known in England, and who had just arrived in Rome.

Lady Westmoreland questioned Severn about his friend, and he, anxious to escape the tentacles of this Medusa, exalted Catherwood's abilities as an architectural draftsman. She then asked Severn if his friend Frederick Catherwood might like to accompany them in her tour of the Nile. 'I have no doubt,' said Joseph Severn (repeating the conversation in a letter home), 'that Mr. Catherwood would feel himself honoured by your ladyship's suggestion. I am distressed, not being able to take advantage of your ladyship's kindness myself, but Mr. Catherwood might go without me.' Momentarily thwarted in her attempt to enmesh Joseph Severn, Lady Westmoreland ended the conversation by saying, 'My Dear Mr. Severn. I do not know this young man, but I would take anyone of your commending, because I feel you understand me.' [6] And with that arrangements were made for the presentation of Mr. Catherwood.

Severn brought Catherwood to the Villa Negroni and presented him to Lady Westmoreland just as she was returning from the ball at the French Embassy. The sight of the still lovely Jane Huck-Saunders, now Lady Westmoreland, in her high-waisted dress of tulle over which lay some shimmering golden material, and her naturally blonde hair festooned with golden osprey feathers, was to Catherwood an enchanting picture. When he was presented, according to Joseph Severn, he completely lost his voice.

When Catherwood found it, he was delighted with the proposal that he go to Egypt in the train of Lady Westmoreland. Joseph Severn advised against it as he related to his sister Maria,

. . . The proposition was made to him . . . & he was very much pleased with the idea. I have persuaded him not to for those Reasons— that it will be infinitely better to remain in Rome and study Architecture such as he has prepared for—on the other hand he thinks this a most favourable opportunity and perhaps the only one of us going to Egypt—and therefore that it should not be suffered to escape— and as Lady W. will have so many servants and such good preparation for the journey—he will go without danger.

Catherwood, like the young man in Balzac's *Les Illusions perdues* was brought suddenly from modest circumstances and plunged into a personal relation with a titled *précieuse;* he was caught as the rest of Roman society in the pedantic fribbles of Lady Westmoreland. Henry Fox wrote,[7]

Her character, would take pages to illustrate—her wonderful talents and brilliant conversation make it impossible not to have pleasure in her society. . . She is perhaps not mad, but nobody ever approached so near it with much reason. . . She divides the world

19

into two classes, her friends and her enemies which supply for her vocabulary the words good and bad . . . the inconsistencies of her character are endless . . . and one might draw it up in perpetual antithesis. . .

Three months after Catherwood met Lady Westmoreland—he became one of the young gentlemen of her coterie, and by December the lady's lover, as Joseph Severn implies in a letter to his sister.

[Catherwood] is living at present in Lady Westmoreland's palace—she is a little fearful of her servants and wanted me to take up my residence there to keep these Italians in order. I was to live with her on my own terms—but I did not like it I am so deeply fixed in my Studies that I think of nothing else. . . Nor will I. . . So I asked Catherwood . . . he liked it much . . . and I proposed him with success . . . so now he has packed up his Art and is Lord and Master . . . at the Villa Negroni.[8]

And there two months later Joseph Severn accompanied by Seymour Kirkup, visited him.

We dined last Sunday with Lady W.—in company with a merry fellow named Kirkupp—[*sic*] an Englishman—all the dinner and after Lady W's talk was tedious so that we were near going frantick—but she made a sudden pause and all were silent when as Ill luck would have it Catherwood's belly set up a loud grumbling and we could not keep our Countenances but we broke out into a laugh. Poor Catherwood's belly. . . But he is going on very well [9]

And so he did for a time. Then came the rupture of the friendship and the menage broke up. Whether Catherwood left her, as most people left Lady Westmoreland highly angered over her mercurial whims, or whether the cuckolded Earl of Westmoreland made an unheralded appearance, Severn, our chronicler, makes no mention. Gone was Catherwood and gone the proposed expedition up the Nile. However, *l'affaire* Westmoreland did have its positive side; it awakened in Catherwood a desire to tour Egypt.

But he was already at work in Rome, trying, in an excess of zeal, to make up for the lost months at the Villa Negroni. For a while he was with the Duchess of Devonshire while she was directing her private excavations in the Forum, and with Henry Parke he made his first archaeological drawings depicting the Catacombs later published in the *Dictionary of Architecture*.[10] Then moving southward with drafting board and easel he went to the two Sicilies.

In the land of Demeter, Catherwood had his first glimpse of the remains of the Greeks. He followed the Eastern shore, all along the way making sketches of the ruins in the effusive and melodious style of the Romantics. Thus he came to the ruins of Taormina. These lie midway between Syracuse and Messina, in the Homeric country where Ulysses and his companions were confined by the Cyclopes and where the nymph Galatea was possessed by Acis. The ruins of a Greek theater excavated twenty-three centuries ago out of the living rock from the northern face of Mount Taor—a section of ancient walls with ruined columns facing Homer's 'purple sea'—was all that remained of Taormina. The scene was stirringly picturesque. In the distance, snow-crowned Mt. Etna acted as a superb backdrop, rising 10,800 feet into the blue Sicilian sky: the fabled Mt. Etna, where the Cumean Sybil abandoned Aeneas in the kingdom of mighty Dis. It was this that Catherwood painted in tempera, 'Mt. Etna from the Ruins of Tauramina.' * It is a *pièce du milieu;* but a superb one. As composition and drawing and in the use of color, it shows him worthy of standing beside such famous early British watercolorists as Rooker, Cox, Cotman, and Harding. When the picture was exhibited in New York at the National Academy of Design in

---

* This picture was exhibited in 1839 at the National Academy of Design in New York and appears as Number 10 'Mount Etna from the Ruins of Tauramina.' It was purchased by Mr. S. S. Swords and has remained in the family for five generations; the present owner is Mrs. Frederic G. Hoppin of New York. They have known it only as 'The Catherwood.'

1839, it drew exaggerated praise from Cole, himself a master of the picturesque. And Thomas Cole remembered that picture. When he went abroad in 1841 and to Sicily, he went to Taormina and painted 'Mount Aetna from Taormina' (1844) from almost the same spot that Catherwood, twenty years before him, had painted his 'Mt. Etna.'

Not many months after Shelley was drowned, and before Lord Byron took his much publicized expedition to Greece, Catherwood, in the autumn of 1822, left for Athens in company with his architectural friends.

After Rome, Greece was for young students the architectural Mecca, for Italy, the first to feel the pulse of archaeology, had given birth in 1733 to the Society of Dilettanti, composed of learned men—mostly Englishmen—who sponsored those superbly illustrated folios on classical architecture. Then the Dilettanti activities spread to Greece. Every artist and architect knew in the eighteenth century of the work of Stuart, Revett, and Chandler among the ruins of Hellas, and the researches of Cockerell, who measured the Doric Acropolis. Yet it was only after Lord Elgin's myrmidons, with mattock and crowbar, plundered the Parthenon and brought back the famous Greek marbles to London that Greece became the mecca of architects. Accompanied by Donaldson and Scoles, Frederick Catherwood went to Athens, arriving just about the moment that Lord Byron, volunteering for service with the Greeks, landed at Missolonghi with his retinue of 12 people, 5 horses, 2 canon, and 50,000 Spanish pesos.

What Catherwood's itinerary was in Greece, or what he precisely drew, we do not know, none of his Grecian drawings having come to light. All we know with certainty is what was succinctly revealed by his friend Stephens: 'Mr. Catherwood . . . shut up in Athens during the Greek revolution when it was beseiged by the Turks, pursued his artistical studies and perforce made castings with his own hands.' [11]

For Catherwood arrived during the war between the Greeks and Turks, who were at each other's throats in a revolution fanned by the flames of religious discord and racial antipathy. In 1821 the Greeks—initiated by the patriotic society Hetaira Philike—began a general uprising. The Turks, handicapped by geography, were at first thrown back throughout Greece. In 1824, while Catherwood was in Athens, the Turks began the offensive. Somehow Catherwood escaped, making his way through the Greek isles into Syria. The Levant was also in flames. Civil war was being waged about the Pashalik of Acre, between Sheik and Emir, and the only refuge for Englishmen, at the time, was in the *dar el Sytt*, the home of Lady Hester Stanhope, the white-robed Sibyl of the Lebanon.[12] But Catherwood and Henry Parke avoided the eccentric Lady Stanhope and, dressed as Arabs, made their way to the Nile.

2

Catherwood arrived in Egypt at the time that 'Egyptianism' was taking hold in European intellectual circles, inspired by the publications of the French savants who had traveled with Napoleon during his short-lived conquest of that land. Beyond the superb beginnings of the Napoleonic architects little systematic work had been undertaken in those vast archaeological ossuaries; it had been only six years since Giovanni Belzoni had broken into the Khafre pyramid where he had pierced the walls and entered the labyrinths, trampling on golden-plated mummies as 'thick, as leaves in Vallambrosa.' Catherwood remembered as a boy seeing post-bills advertising Belzoni as 'The Patagonia Sampson,' which exhibited his herculean six-foot-six-inch frame. Yet the archaeological bug having bitten Belzoni, he, after performing for many years in the circus, saved enough money to descend on Egypt and rip open the sealed tombs of the Pharaohs. So early was Catherwood on the Egyptian scene that he arrived there the same year that Champollion, using the Rosetta stone as the key, was publishing his *Précis.**

In Cairo there were many young Englishmen who aided and protected by His Majesty's Consul the most expeditious Henry Salt, were busily exploring Egypt. Young Wilkinson, who was to become one of the most famous Egyptologists and enter the lists as Sir John Gardner Wilkinson, was already at Thebes working among the tombs with James Haliburton. In Cairo, Catherwood and his companions found Humphreys, Fox-Strangways, the accomplished Major Felix, the Frenchman Linant (who was to earn enduring fame for his explorations with the Marquis León de la Borde at the Nabatean ruins of Petra), Lord Prudhoe and Robert Hay, all at work, in one way or another, on Egyptian antiquities.

In the autumn of 1824 Frederick Catherwood, in company with Henry Parke and Joseph Scoles, hired a vessel and went up the Nile. Drawing and sketching on the way, they went a thousand miles beyond the first cataracts into the Nubian country. There at considerable risk of life, for pencil and paper were accursed to the Arab, these young architects systematically mapped the clusters of ruins in the Upper Nile. In more than one sense Catherwood's career was cast in Egypt, for in October 1824 at Alexandria, he met Robert Hay, a titled young man who later conducted the first systematic explorations of the Nilotic remains. Hay had not as yet made his first journey when he met Catherwood and Henry Parke. It was Catherwood's drawings that delighted and raised his enthusiasm ('if that is possible,' writes Robert Hay) and determined his interest in Egyptology. On 4 October,

---

* *Précis du systéme hiéroglyphique des anciens Egyptiéns,* by Jean François Champollion, Paris, 1824.

Robert Hay dined with Catherwood 'who gave him,' as he writes in his own unpublished autobiography, 'much good information on Egypt.' [13] This meeting, as the sequel will reveal, was to make archaeological history.

Three years of travel having taken all of Catherwood's money, he proposed to return to England, with his portfolio of drawings, and recoup. He could not have selected a worse time to cross the Mediterranean, with the war raging between Greece and Turkey. Fortunately for him, however, he left Egypt ('on an Austrian brig that proposes going from Alexandria to Zante [dropping] Catherwood who proceeds to Greece,' wrote Robert Hay), before the combined French and British fleets annihilated the galleys of Mehemet Ali; lives of Englishmen after that were not highly esteemed by the Pasha. But Catherwood cleared the Mediterranean before the blow fell, picked up the casts of Grecian sculpture he had made previously, and made his way to Rome on his way back to England. This much we know. Joseph Severn, writing to his family from Rome in December 1825 said, 'Catherwood arrived. He will give you all particulars about me.' [14]

3

The estimable Mr. Catherwood arrived in an England torn by multiple dissensions: corn, currency, and Catholics, as Philip Guedalla puts it—the social effects of the industrial revolution. Catherwood walked right into the first Reform Riots. Watt's improved steam engine, Hargreave's powered spinning wheels, Maudslay lathes, Cartwright's powerloom were already fashioning England into one gigantic factory. The noises of the new machine-mythology mixing with the old cries of London—the bell of the postman, the bawl of the water-cart man—were a cacophony to the artist-architect returning from a land of silence.

Pre-Victorian society—and with it, Catherwood—was tossed into a maelstrom.

In this economic confusion Catherwood attempted to carry on his profession. He designed, we know, a large glass house built near Westminster Bridge, and some workers' houses at Pentonville; [15] pressed for money he sold some of his sketches to the Egyptian Hall at Piccadilly, which had been built in 1823 during his absence. But apparently things did not go very well with him and he must have often thought of the life—the exciting creative life—he had left in Egypt. Although he exhibited again at the Royal Academy [16] (the architectural drawings he had made in Egypt) there seemed nothing to hold him in London. When at the end of 1828 he received an offer from Robert Hay, who asked him to return to Egypt, Catherwood quickly dropped his T-square and compass and made ready to depart. At the age of twenty-nine Catherwood began the second phase of his career.

On his way to Egypt he passed through Italy and stopped for some days in Rome; Joseph Severn wrote his brother: '*New Year's Day 1829* . . . I heard from Catherwood the other day.'

4

Robert Hay of Linplum, heir to the marquisate of Tweed-dale, after exploring the Nile for some years, had thought out a most ambitious archaeological program. With a retinue of experienced artists, architects, topographical draftsmen, and antiquarians (they were not yet archaeologists), Robert Hay planned to go up the Nile and investigate each ruined site, known and unknown. At each he planned to have his artists draw the murals with their inscriptions, and to have the architects make ground plans of the ruins. It was to be the greatest scientific expedition since Napoleon, between the years 1799-1801, came to Egypt with his army of conquest and a regiment of savants. Robert Hay's expedition was composed of a company of Englishmen, many of whom in later years became famous for one reason or another. The group included: Joseph Bonomi, Francis Arundale, James Haliburton (called Burton), Charles Laver, Edward W. Lane and Wilkinson (two incipient Egyptologists), G. B. Greenough, George A. Hoskins, and, to end the impressive list, Frederick Catherwood. These young men, during the years 1828-38, were to lay down a systematic basis of Egyptian archaeology.

Catherwood had first heard of Robert Hay in London when he attended the architectural lectures at the Royal Academy. He was the grandson of John Hay, the First Earl of Tweeddale, famous for the speech in Edinburgh that launched the Scots Colony at Darien. With seemingly small interest in the title he would one day inherit from his brother, Robert Hay was destined to spend most of his life in the Near East, and to marry, much to the chagrin of the editor of *Burke's Peerage*, Kalitza, daughter of Alexander Psaraké, chief magistrate of Apodulo at Crete. Still Hay used his inheritance to good purpose; at his own expense, he maintained this large expedition, which remained in the field for more than ten years. He bequeathed to the British Museum forty-nine folio volumes of paintings, drawings, plans, and panoramas of Egyptian antiquities, a monument of archaeological research.[17] He published, however, but a single book.

The expedition began its work at Memphis, the gateway to the glory of ancient Egypt, drawing to scale the great pyramids of Giza-Khufu, Khafre, and Menkawre, a work in which Catherwood, for one, was engaged for some time. And remembered, too, for Catherwood's sketch of the pyramids of Gizeh was published. After Memphis, Sakkareh; then it was Abydos; by 1832, the expedition was one thousand miles up the Nile and had set up its camp among the ruins of Thebes.

It was here at the ruins of the greatest cities of the ancient world—Thebes, Karnak, Luxor, and Deir el Bahri—that Robert

Hay's expeditionists devoted their greatest attention. The magnificent temples built in the time of Queen Hatshepsut in 1500 B.C. (under the architectural guidance of Sen-Mut) crowded the banks of the Nile. The Temple of Karnak, composed of red granite cut at quarries at Aswan, was so beautiful when completed that it brought insomnia to Hatshepsut, who said that 'she would not sleep because of this temple.' It had virtually the same effect upon the young English architects who pitched their tents among these superbly beautiful monuments of violently polychromed limestone.

Catherwood began work in September 1832 and, after careful measurements drew first a colored plan of Thebes and then a detailed plan of the whole ruins. He then worked on a panorama of the valley showing Thebes—a sketch that would one day be enlarged into a huge scenic panorama and displayed in London and New York. Later he drew to scale the obelisks [18] that protruded their stone tongues above the ruins. Joseph Bonomi, who displayed great skill in rendering hieroglyphics, drew the interiors of the Theban tombs, the murals, and inscriptions from the tomb of Rekhmare. In the meanwhile Charles Laver was working on Karnak, making a rough plan of the superb capital of Amen-Hotep III.

The apogee of Egyptian architecture was reached in Amen-Hotep's sanctuary at Amūn, enlarged later by the Ramesses. This was fully realized by Robert Hay, for he assigned Francis Arundale to make views, plans, and sections of the principal buildings [19] of Karnak, Luxor, the temples of Medinet Habu, Gourna, and the surrounding region; Joseph Bonomi kept to the hieroglyphics.

Toward the end of 1833 Catherwood, in company with James Haliburton, began work on the 'Colossi of Memnon.' Haliburton—of the Haliburtons of Roxburgshire—had come to Egypt in 1821 with Wilkinson, at the invitation of Mehemet Ali, to make a geological survey of the Nile. There, falling under the spell of the *antique*, he soon left the employ of the Pasha and went up the Nile. He had published in Cairo several bulky folios entitled *Excerpta Hieroglyphica* [20] and was known thereafter as an authority in the glyphic art. But he published little more; his personal history, like that of Catherwood, is lost.

On the west bank of the Nile, between the ruined structure Medinet Habu and the Ramesseum, with its feet eternally lapped by the rising Nile, stood the seventy-foot high statue of Amen-Hotep III. An architectural sculpture three thousand years old, it had been fashioned out of a reddish conglomerate from the sand-hills of Edfu, floated down the Nile in eight especially constructed ships. Overawed by the size and grandeur of his work, the architect-sculptor of the 'Colossi' glowed with enthusiasm; 'They are wonderful,' he said in hieroglyphics, 'for size and height, and they will last as long as heaven.'

Catherwood raised a scaffold on the battered faceless sides of statues, measured in detail, these wonderful monuments of the 'vocal Memnon,' and drew them to scale, and then he excavated about their base and discovered that they reposed only on a stratum of sand. Catherwood's drawings, the first accurate ones ever made, were never published; they lie in the anonymity of the Hay collections in the British Museum.[21] But his drawing of the Ramesseum Court, the raised terrace and the Osiris pillars of Ramesses II, had a published history; this appeared in Finden's *Landscape Illustrations of the Bible*.

The expedition continued up the Nile, working at Hierakonpolis, Edfu, and finally about Elephantine and the Isle of Philae at the first cataract of the Nile. There Catherwood copied the inscriptions on the intaglio walls relating to Ptolemy and Cleopatra.[22] After many months in the temples of Philae, the beauty of which had once made Pierre Loti weep, Catherwood drew, among others, a watercolor that he thought was good enough to retain; * the expedition then passed on above the Aswan cataracts and entered Nubia. After some weeks in Nubia, where Catherwood helped the other members of the expedition to delineate the ruins,[23] he left with Francis Arundale and returned to Cairo. There they prepared for an expedition into Arabia Petra.

5

Years in the Near East, under the benign action of the Mediterranean sun, had brought about an outward change in the appearance of Frederick Catherwood. He dressed as an Arab, with robe and turban, and, so says his friend Arundale, 'he was well versed in Oriental manners' and could speak fluent Arabic, Italian, and Hebrew; he seems also to have lost something of the reticence that early characterized him. By 1833 he had accumulated a great mass of material and he had given himself a training such as few architect-archaeologists had up to that time—or perhaps since. He had not only traveled the classical lands, Italy, Greece, and Sicily, delineating with considerable skill their ancient structures, but after his journeys on the Nile he had been employed as an engineer by the redoubtable Mehemet Ali to repair the mosques at Cairo.[24] This permitted him to make the first architectural analyses of saracenic structures, although these drawings, unhappily, are lost. This placed him in favor with Mehemet Ali and he carried the Pasha's personal firman. His experience had not been limited to the mosques, for he traveled through Libya into West Africa, and in 1832 he was at the Regency of Tunis at Dugga, where he drew a twenty-foot plinth, a beautiful four-columned prostyle of the Corinthian order, built of the limestone of the country, with an inscription on its façade stating that it had been erected by two brothers: *L. M. Simplex and S. M. Simplex Re-*

---

* 297 Island of Philae, First cataract of the Nile—*Moonlight;* exhibited in 1845 at the National Academy of Design, New York.

gilian built at their own expense in honour of Jupiter and Minerva during the reign of Marcus Aurelius and his colleague in empire L. Aurelius Verus.[25] It is well that Catherwood drew this Roman monument when he did, for in 1847 Sir Thomas Reade, British Consul at Tunis, completely destroyed it when he tried to remove the inscription. That Temple at Dugga left a profound impression on Catherwood, for even after he had become famed as the co-discoverer of the Mayan civilization, his paper for the American Ethnological Society, the second piece he published, was, strangely enough, on this monument.[26] And, apparently, it had interest for art historians too, for James Fergusson, the famous historian of architecture, used Catherwood's drawing, as did the great Dr. F. H. W. Gesenius in his *Monumenta Phoenicia.*[27]

In August 1833 Catherwood, Arundale, and Bonomi, dressed as Turkish merchants, completed their preparations for an expedition into Arabia Petra. The record of this journey, as one might now suspect, is not supplied by the reticent Mr. Catherwood but by his friend, Francis Arundale.[28] Younger than Catherwood by eight years, Arundale had been a pupil of the elder Augustus Pugin —Gothicist. Articled out to him for seven years, he had gone to France with his master, where he assisted in the drawings of Pugin's *Architectural Antiquities of Normandy.* Arundale's unhandsome face was dominated by a large nose and a large head, prematurely balding, which fact he tried to hide by combing his hair in a wild windswept fashion. It almost seemed that his florid name, Francis Vyvyan Jago Arundale, was an attempt to balance his ugliness. His archaeological work with Robert Hay in Egypt was, unfortunately for his reputation, never published. After nine adventurous years in the Levant, he married, became the father of six children, and published one book.

For the expedition into Edom they purchased, wrote Arundale, 'necessaries from the bazaar at Cairo; and the day of departure being fixed for August 29, 1833—the morning was all activity.' They left, at the time of the evening prayers, with nine camels, slowly proceeding through the bazaars, following the direct route to Suez. They followed the camel road alongside of the Red Sea, and passing the 'Written Mountain'—the Mokatteb rock of inscriptions—they entered the Wadi Feiran and arrived at the Convent of St. Catherine. After climbing Mt. Sinai, which Catherwood sketched, they started across the desert on 20 September, bound for Gaza. By October they reached Jerusalem.

The ancient battle-scarred lands of Palestine, Syria, and Transjordania now became the crucible of Catherwood's archaeological research. Camouflaged as a Turk who could, when pressed, display the firman of the Pasha of Egypt, with his drawing board and camera lucida * carried by an Arab, Catherwood surveyed the cities of the Decacopolis. He moved among the ruined sites of Gadara, an adornment in the time of Roman dominion, and toured Roman Gerasa in Transjordania. At Gerasa, where the ancient stone thoroughfares battled with vegetation and time, Catherwood measured the Temple of Artemis and drew the remains of its amphitheater with its column-bound Forum. Moving northward, with a camel-train for conveyance and Francis Arundale as a companion, he went through Damascus into Lebanon. The fertile field of the Valley of the Lebanon, enclosed by cypress and cedar, had held, ever since the dimmest antiquity, civilizations of many forms; and the glittering archaeological crown of the valley was the ruins of Baalbec. Pitching his tent among the fallen, lavishly carved columns, Catherwood, with Arundale in attendance, began the survey of the once mighty Temple of Jupiter-Baal. With careful attention to detail Catherwood drew the architectural lyrics of Baalbec, the Propylaea, the forecourt, the Great Forecourt with its altar pure and pristinely classical, the

---

* The camera lucida was an instrument, much used in the nineteenth century for copying the outlines of buildings by means of a prism, formed by a peculiar arrangement of mirrors it causes an external image to be projected on a sheet of paper so that its outlines can be traced.

Heliopolis-Temple of Jupiter-Baal, and the sections of the Temple of Baachus with its exquisite stone doorway and motif of fig leaves that time and man had spared. It had been erected in the era of Antonio Pius (86-161), pillaged in 748 by the Seljuka, fell in 1134 into the blood-stained hands of Jenghiz Khan, and was taken by the Turks in 1517, in whose territory it remained until 1918.

With proud dignity the six remaining columns of the Temple of Jupiter, 62 feet in height, commanded the panorama of the watered greenness. The beautiful temple of the Romans, turned into a basilica by the Byzantines, transformed by the Moslems into a mosque, and destroyed by the Mongols, was now only the winter stall for nomadic shepherds. Yet history still flowed around the ruins; Lady Hester Stanhope had traveled to it in 1814 in search for treasure in the cists of the great plain of Baal, and it had been visited by many antiquarians who lamented in Volneyesque accents the transcience of empires. Norman Douglas has written a book, *Love Among the Ruins*, about the Baalbec ruins. But it was Catherwood who first made them widely known. Although his drawings of it were not published, his sketches were made into a huge panoramic canvas and exhibited in many of the world's principal cities.[29]

It was, however, in Jerusalem at the Dome of the Rock and at the Mosque of El-'Aqsá, those saracenic masterpieces known generally as The Mosque of Omar, that Catherwood completed his most important work in the Near East.

When the Arabs swept into the Jordan Valley, overwhelming the armies of Heraclitus, all Palestine fell. The Arabs entered Jerusalem A.D. 640. Behind the ancient city wall—the lower courses of which belonged to the period of Herod the Great—the Arabs, with the aid of Greek Christian architects and workmen, erected the magnificent Dome of the Rock. It and the adjoining Mosque of El-'Aqsá were built in A.D. 691 by the Umaiyad prince Abd el-Malik.

The Dome of the Rock had long been a subject of heated dispute between contending antiquarians, architects, and religious historians. A mosaic-walled mosque in a corner of ancient Jerusalem, it has long held a place in the Islamic diadem. For here Mohammed, so runs the legend, escorted by the Archangel Gabriel, ascended on his eagle-winged horse to visit the seven heavens of Islam. Mohammed's footprint is supposed to be impressed in that sacred black rock, a fact on which Mark Twain cast much impish doubt when he measured it and judged that Mohammed would have taken a size 18 shoe. In Catherwood's day, unbelievers took their lives in their hands when they entered those sacred portals. No architect up to that time had ever sketched its architecture, no antiquarian had traced its interior design. Catherwood could no longer resist it; on 13 November 1833, dressed as an Egyptian officer and carrying, as he wrote, a 'strong firman expressly naming me an engineer in the service of Mehemet Ali,' Catherwood, with his drawing materials, entered the Mosque. He was accompanied by a servant 'of great courage and assurance who, coming from Egypt, held the canaille of Jerusalem in the extreme of contempt.' In this single instance of Catherwood's amazing career he has left a personal account.[30] After making a survey of Jerusalem and a general plan of Harm es Shereef,[31] and drawings of the exteriors of El-'Aqsá and the Dome of the Rock, he entered the interior of the Mosque 'feeling irresistibly urged to make an attempt to explore them.' Catherwood returned with his camera lucida and sat down to make a drawing. He wrote:

It was a proceeding certain to attract attention of the most indifferent and expose me to dangerous consequences. The cool assurance of my servant, at once befriended and led me on. We entered, and arranging the camera, I quickly sat down to my work, not without some nervousness, as I perceived the Mussulmen, from time to time, mark me with doubtful looks; however, most of them passed on, deceived by my dress and the quiet indifference with which I regarded them. At length some, more fanatic than the rest, began to think all could not be right; they gathered at a distance in groups, suspiciously eyeing me, and comparing notes with one another; a storm was evidently gathering. They approached, broke into sudden clamour, and surrounding us, uttered loud curses; their numbers increased most alarmingly, and with their numbers their menacing language and gestures. Escape was hopeless; I was completely surrounded by a mob of two hundred people who seemed screwing up their courage for a sudden rush upon me—I need not tell you what would have been my fate. Nothing could be better than the conduct of Suleyman, my servant, at this crisis; affecting vast indignation at the interruption, he threatened to inform the Governor, out-hectored the most clamorous, and raising his whip, actually commenced a summary attack upon them, and knocked off the cap of one of the holy dervishes. This brought matters to a crisis; and, I believe, few moments would have passed ere we had been torn to pieces, when an incident occurred that converted our danger and discomfiture into positive triumph. This was the sudden appearance of the Governor on the steps of the platform, accompanied by his usual train. Catching sight of him, the foremost—those I mean who had been disgraced by the blows of Suleyman—rushed tumultuously up to him, demanding the punishment of the infidel, who was profaning the holy precincts, and horse-whipping the true believers. At this the Governor drew near, and as we had often smoked together, and were well acquainted, he saluted me politely, and supposing it to be beyond the reach of possibility that I could venture to do what I was about without warrant from the pasha, he at once applied himself to cool the rage of the mob. 'You see, my friends,' he said, 'that our holy mosque is in a dilapidated state, and no doubt our lord and master Mehemet Ali has sent this Effendi to survey it, in order to complete its repair. If we are unable to do these things for ourselves, it is right to employ those who can; and such being the will of our lord, the pasha, I require you to disperse and not incur my displeasure by any further interruption.' And turning to me, he said, in hearing of them all, that if anyone had the hardihood to disturb me in the future, he would deal in a summary way with him. I did not, of course, think it necessary to undeceive the worthy Governor; and gravely thanking him, proceeded with my drawing. All went on quietly after this.

During six weeks, I continued to investigate every part of the mosque and its precincts.[32] Introducing my astonished companions as necessary assistants in the work of the survey. But when I heard of the near approach of *Ibrahim Pasha*, I thought it was time to take leave of Jerusalem. The day after my departure, he entered, and as it happened, several English travellers of distinction arrived * at the same time. Anxious to see the mosque, they asked permission of Ibrahim, whose answer was characteristic of the man, to the purport, that they were welcome to go if they liked, but he would not insure their safe return, and that he could not venture to outrage the feelings of the Mussulmen, by sending an escort with them. Here he was met with the story of my recent visit. He said it was impossible; the dervishes were summoned; the governor was summoned, and an *eclaircissement* took place, which must have been a scene of no small amusement.

It was more than simple curiosity that urged this rash attempt, and its fortunate issue enabled me, with my associates, to make a complete and scientific survey of the mosques, vaults, gateways, and other objects comprised within the extent of the area. . .

So Catherwood—with the assistance of Arundale and Bonomi—continued to draw the mosque. They made sections of the dome, measuring the exterior walls and the sweep of the walls. Within six weeks Catherwood had enough details of the most famous mosque in the whole Mohammedan world to erect another like it. Catherwood's art had reached its apogee; it was his greatest single work. He had intended on his return to London to publish his work in book form, utilizing all the superb drawings that he had made. But the London publishers, for one reason or another, were indifferent; in disgust Catherwood put hi. drawings away. They were published throughout the following years only in fragments. Not many years after Catherwood had worked there, violent controversy developed between various schools of architecture over the origin of the Dome of the Rock. Mr. James Fergusson, the eminent historian of architecture, conjectured that

---

* Francis Arundale states they were the Marquis of Waterford, Sir William Geary, and William Bagot (2nd Baron Bagot), members of the House of Lords.

this mosque had been built by Constantine over the tomb of Christ. Challenged by antiquarians, he sought out Catherwood, to see the drawings and prove his archaeology theory. In 1846 he made contact with him: 'The only means,' Fergusson wrote, 'that occurred to me of getting out of this dilemma was trying if possible to gain access to Mr. Catherwood's drawings which I knew from the works of Dr. Robinson and Mr. [W. H.] Bartlett did exist somewhere. Mr. Catherwood was then in Demerara [British Guiana] and in answer to a letter I wrote him he gave me hope he would accede to my wishes when he returned to this country which he did last autumn [1846] . . .' In January 1847 Catherwood turned over his collection of drawings to Fergusson and persuaded Francis Arundale, who was on the point of death, to do likewise; 'they agreed' acknowledged James Fergusson, 'to turn over the material in a handsome manner.' [33] Thus disappeared one phase of Catherwood's own archaeological monument; giving his drawings one by one to interested scholars, he lost his identity.[34] Now all his drawings of the Mosque of Omar have disappeared.

Chapter Four

ROBERT BURFORD'S PANORAMA

In the last years of the reign of King William IV, Great Britain was poised to enter an unprecedented era of material prosperity; to take advantage of it Frederick Catherwood returned to London. And into business. The years of unprofitable research amid the ruins of ancient cultures had brought Catherwood neither fame nor riches. Inspired by the need of money he entered business— as a panoramist; he mortgaged his art services to Robert Burford and his Panoramas in Leicester Square.

Leicester Square had long been the center of panoramic attractions. Its out-sized rotundas housing colossal circular murals, paintings of battles, coronations, cities remote and romantic drew, as does the cinema today, immense numbers of curious people. This cloud of panoramas, dioramas, poluphusikons, and eidophusikons, 'where the eye was pleased without the brain being duly exerted,' [1] had a great hold on the public, not only in London but in all the other world metropolises. It was an art form that held the public interest for more than a half a century, until P. T. Barnum reached the heights of absurdity by allowing 'real water' to flow out of a panorama of the Niagara Falls. Although many of art's immortals painted panoramas at one time or other in their careers, little is known about the medium. The panorama has had a neglected history. [2]

Herr Breisig, a German architectural painter of Danzig, is credited with the idea of the panorama in the late eighteenth century. It was soon taken up with much profit by Robert Barker of Edinburgh, who went to London in 1793 with his sketch of a panorama of Edinburgh. He gained admission to Sir Joshua Reynolds' studio and exhibited his plan. Reynolds, whose gout weighed as much upon him as his honors, snorted that a continuous cylindrical muralistic canvas 100 feet long and 10 in height was wholly impractical. Yet when challenged and pressed by the visionary Scot, Reynolds promised, provided it was not exhibited too far away, that he would visit it to see if Robert Barker had succeeded. With the financial aid of Lord Elcho, the arts-loving son of the Earl of Nemyss, Barker erected a rotunda at 28 Castle Street, Leicester Square. As promised, Sir Joshua appeared, making the circle of Barker's mural, shuffling about in his bedroom slippers. He approved. So did the public. Always avid for anything that would dissipate the perpetual ennui of the city, the people patronized Barker's panoramas to the extent that he built another rotunda on Cranbourne Street.

Leicester Square had been well chosen as a site for the panoramas. It had a long art tradition. Sir Joshua Reynolds had lived there since 1760, painting in his Leicester Square studio the portraits that had made him famous. Hogarth, his contemporary, had lived nearby at the Sign of the Golden Head until his death, and a certain exotic air continued to bring artists to the Square. Long a favorite resort for duelists it became also a home for French Huguenots after the revocation of the Edict of Nantes. Peter the Great had been entertained there when he came to England, in 1698, to learn shipbuilding, and this atmosphere of the foreigner continued to the end of the century when aristocratic emigrés, fleeing the revolution, took refuge in the *pensions* facing the Square—the Square named after Robert Sindet, the Second Earl of Leicester.

So apparent was this 'foreign air' that Charles Dickens in *Bleak House* complained of it as 'a centre of attraction to indifferent foreign hotels and indifferent foreigners, Old China, gaming houses, exhibitions and a large medley of shabbiness and drinking out of sight.' And 'sex shops, too,' writes the author of the *En-cyclopædia of London*, 'sex shops, birth control devices by Mrs. Philips,' announced at 5 Orange Street near Leicester Fields at the Sign of the Golden Fan and Rising Sun, where she 'sells implements of safety having thirty-five years' experience in making them and selling them.' [3] Decidedly, Leicester Square was well chosen for Robert Barker's Panoramas!

In the Rotunda, designed by Robert Mitchell, who later published a volume on this unusually lighted building,[4] the people of London saw a muralistic history of their times. Whenever some noteworthy event occurred, Barker sent his own son or other artists attached to the panorama to make sketches, and within the time of memory a large, dramatically lighted panorama was set up in the rotunda. The medium became so popular that many famed British artists, at one time or other in their apprenticeship, contributed to the panoramas; Thomas Girtin, the famous English watercolorist was one of these.* Although Robert Barker patented his panorama under the title of 'La Nature à Coup d'Oeil,' it did not prevent a flood of imitations. Sir Ashton Lever brought together a collection of natural history specimens from his 'cabinet,' put them before a mural background, and called it the 'Holophusicon,' but it was called 'The Leverian Museum' by the general public. Loutherbourg, the dropcurtain painter of Covent Garden, made a mechanical panorama—an 'Eidophusikon'—moved by machinery, which produced varied effects, sunshine, gloom, rain, storm.[5] Gainsborough, who was a spectator, was unaccountably thrilled; 'He could,' the account runs, 'talk of nothing else.' By 1830 the number of exhibits had so expanded that Coghlan's

---

* 'Panorama of London' by Thomas Girtin, exhibited 27 August 1802 'Eido-metropolis, a great panoramic picture of London, Westminster, and Environs, now exhibiting at the Great Room, Spring Garden. Admission 1/s.' The Print Room in the British Museum has the original sketches of Girtin's panorama.

Cicerone, or Fashionable Guide to all Places of Public Amusement could list Dioramas in Regent's Park, Cosmoramas in Regent Street, and an Apollonicon in St. Martin's Lane, where scenes, 'painted solid and in transparence arranged so as to exhibit changes of light and shade,' thrilled the public. Still Barker's Panorama held the center of the stage.

On Robert Barker's death, his son Henry, who had been trained at the Royal Academy, acquired the panoramas. It was he who made the sketches of Edinburgh from Carlton Hill from which his father executed the first panorama. It was a profitable enterprise under Henry Ashton Barker. He exhibited huge panoramic canvases of Turkey, Constantinople, the Battle of Waterloo, the coronation procession of George IV in 1822, and many others of which there is ample record. Barker even wanted to make a panorama of the Mutiny of the Bounty, but after he married Harriet, the daughter of Admiral William Bligh, he dropped the subject. In 1826 Barker turned over his interests to the Burfords. father and son, and thereafter the rotunda in Leicester Square was known as 'Robert Burford's Panorama.'

Robert Burford, who trained Frederick Catherwood as a panoramist, had been actively engaged in the enterprise ever since he had left the study rooms of the Royal Academy. An excellent artist—and much traveled—he made the original sketches for the panoramic murals of Waterloo, Athens, Niagara Falls, Constantinople, Ruins of Pompeii, and in 1830 the View of New York City.[6] In constant search for new material, Burford sought out British artists as they returned from their tours. So in 1835 he got in touch with Frederick Catherwood, newly arrived from the Holy Land. Unable to publish his drawings of Jerusalem in any other fashion, Catherwood allowed them to be used for the panorama. It is not clear if Catherwood actually painted the 'Panorama of Jerusalem' although he is known to have assisted in the archaeological details of the buildings. In an autobiographical gesture 'he painted himself and Joseph Bonomi in oriental dress' in the mural. 'Jerusalem' was his first mural. After that followed 'Thebes' and 'Karnak' and the 'Ruins of Baalbec.'[7] If this did not enhance his reputation as an architect it at least provided him with money and gave him courage to marry. It also gave his career direction; it brought him in contact with John Lloyd Stephens.

Stephens, a young American lawyer who had gone to Europe ostensibly for his health, had traveled through Greece, Turkey, Russia, and Poland, and then suddenly had reversed the field and gone to Egypt. He traveled up the Nile, crossed the Red Sea, and followed Catherwood's trail to Mt. Sinai, crossing the dreaded Edom deserts to the intaglio city of Petra. In Jerusalem, a year after Catherwood left for London, Stephens was guided about the Holy Land by a map executed by 'F. Catherwood.' He had seen that name Catherwood etched on Egyptian monuments, and signed in convent registers. In London, in 1836, he met Catherwood at Burford's Panorama, lecturing before his own mural on Jerusalem. This was the beginning of a friendship that was to endure for twenty years. It also would bring about the rediscovery of the Mayan civilization.*

---

* *Maya Explorer: John Lloyd Stephens and the Lost Cities of Central America and Yucatán*, by Victor Wolfgang von Hagen, University of Oklahoma Press, Norman, 1947.

Chapter Five

LITTLE NEW NEW-YORK

In the New York of 1836, Frederick Catherwood encountered little difficulty in finding employment in his profession. Much of lower Manhattan was in a building frenzy trying to replace its losses after the disastrous fire of the previous year.[1] A business card, still preserved, announces:

F. CATHERWOOD,

𝕬𝖗𝖈𝖍𝖎𝖙𝖊𝖈𝖙,

NO. 4 WALL-STREET,

NEW-YORK.

Later Catherwood went into partnership with another architect, Frederick Diaper, and circulars sent throughout the city announced:

The Subscribers [Catherwood & Diaper] respectfully inform their friends that they have entered into arrangements to carry on together the profession of Architects and Surveyors in the City of New York. Their office for the present is at No. 94 Greenwich Street.

Their claims to public favor are:—

43

Mr. Catherwood, Fellow of the Institute of British Architects and F.R.A.S., has in the course of his studies as an Architect visited Italy, Greece, Egypt, France, Germany, England &c. in which countries he has measured and drawn many of the principal remains of ancient magnificence as well as the more important and striking modern edifices. His studies have been pursued during between 7 and 8 years with the greatest perseverance and zeal.

Mr. Diaper was a pupil of Sir Robert Smirke one of the principal Architects to the English Government and has consequently had the most favorable opportunities of seeing and assisting in the construction and superintendence of the great works that have been recently executed and that are now in progress in the English Capitol. The Subscribers are willing to design and superintend the erection of Public Buildings, Houses in Town or Country, Ornamental villas, and the laying out grounds—and to undertake all that appertains to the Science of Architecture and Land Surveying.

Catherwood & Diaper

Frederick Diaper, who, with hypochondriacal care prolonged his life for almost a century, was an accomplished architect. Born in Devonshire, Diaper was articled out to Sir Robert Smirke in London, and later, when he reached his architectural majority, was elected a Fellow of the Royal Institute of British Architects. He was a draftsman in the classical manner and responsible for many buildings in Wall Street—the Bank of America, Union Bank, City Bank, Phoenix Bank. All were done in a rigid classical style; any bank so fashioned seemed to possess the outward habiliments of financial integrity. But it was after Diaper built Delmonico's Hotel, the New York Hotel, and the Society Library that he turned to the building of stately mansions for New York's plutocracy: William Aspinwall's residence; a thirty-room house for August Belmont; an imposing edifice for Daniel Parish, and later a mansion for the father-in-law of Jay Gould. He was classical in style when he built the upstate manor for the 'Good Patroon' Stephen Van Rensselaer, and a home at Fishkill for Gulian C.

Verplanck; thus honored with commissions and emoluments, Frederick Diaper lived on until his ninety-sixth year.[2] All this might have been Catherwood's destiny had he been of the same temperament. Instead, however, Catherwood's enthusiastic unrest sent him to new fields. He, like his friend, Diaper, had been elected while still in England to an Honorary and Corresponding Fellowship to the R.I.B.A.[3] Yet this honor, in America, at least, did not bring any immediate financial change, for Catherwood still dreamed of creating his own Panorama. In anticipation of realizing it, he had brought with him to America the canvas of the 'Panorama of Jerusalem.' That the panorama project was not easily realized we learn from his old friend, James Davies, who wrote him from London in October 1836. He had heard . . .

> . . . most discouraging reports which were in circulation about the complete failure of [Catherwood's] panorama. I was very glad to have all doubts set at rest by your own sign manual. The price of the ground sufficient for your purpose appears most stupendous * but I suppose it is very central and will soon repay the outlay. . . I cannot say that I am astonished at the apathy of the N. Yorkers toward your spec.[iality] . . . they patronize nothing that does not appeal to the passions—actors, singers and mountebanks of all sorts are perfectly deified among them but a beautiful picture is at a 'tarnation discount.'
>
> . . . I admire your idea of giving lectures . . . & think they might be made a very preparatory stuff before opening the panorama . . . you ought to have your head & portfolio too, full of reminiscences of all sorts . . . dont forget to tell them Woolf's story of the crocodiles & Crabs . . . as its something uncommonly in their way and would tickle a youthful audience who were not over nice. . . Since you left, my esposa has given me another Girl. I . . . Trust that you will enjoy the same blessing shortly. . . I hope you and yours are well. I should have liked to have felt more interest in the augury—but the honor

---

* 'One hundred and thirty-eight dollars and eighteen cents ($138.18) the month for a piece of land on Prince Street and Broadway as paid to William Backhouse Astor.' From Catherwood's account book in the collection of New-York Historical Society.

of your wife's acquaintance being thought too great for your old friend—he can only say *vive la bagatelle.*

While the panorama project developed, Catherwood widened his interests; leaving his family * installed in a house at 466 Houston Street, he moved along the New England coast, lecturing when the opportunity presented itself, designing houses when he found commissions. It was at this time, in 1837, that he entered the controversy over the Newport Tower. Catherwood had carried a letter of introduction to Dr. Thomas Webb from John R. Bartlett, the senior partner of Bartlett & Welford's Astor House Book Shop, and Webb commissioned Catherwood to draw five views of the ancient enigmatical round stone tower that stood in what is now Touro Park, Newport, Rhode Island. The tower had been the subject, for more than two centuries, of a great controversy. The 'most unique and puzzling single building in the United States,' as Philip Ainsworth Means wrote; [5] it is thought to hold the key to an unknown portion of America's pre-history. It is believed by some to be 'part of a medieval Catholic church, built by Norsemen, who came to this country between the XIIth and XIVth centuries'; by others merely a part of windmill by Governor Benedict Arnold in 1675. In 1829 the celebrated Danish antiquarian, Professor Karl Christian Rafn, in the process of preparing an exhaustive study of the Norsemen, wrote to the Rhode Island Historical Society seeking information. He asked if there were any traces of the Vikings within the state. Dr. Webb copied for him the abracadabra from the famous Dighton Rock. When Rafn's *Antiquitates Americanae* appeared in 1837, wherein it was stated unequivocally that America was discovered in the tenth

---

* There is but one other record of Catherwood's wife. Her name is never mentioned, not even by John Lloyd Stephens, who would have known her intimately. This much is certain, she was an English woman, she bore Catherwood one child, a son, in London, and another child in America. Letters to John R. Bartlett of the famous Bartlett & Welford Astor House Bookshop give only the bare threads of information. [4]

century by the Norsemen, Dr. Webb thought again about the round stone tower and pondered its origin; it was then that he employed Catherwood. These drawings of the Newport Tower were sent to Professor Rafn, and Catherwood's drawings were engraved in a now famous work [6] and reproduced repeatedly in the century. But the Newport Tower drawings proved to be poor publicity for Catherwood.* After Newport and the tower, Catherwood tried his hand at churches in Boston and New York, and several buildings for the shipping firm of Howland and Aspinwall.

Catherwood's consuming interest remained, however, the panorama. As the project grew in complexity and cost he entered into another partnership, this time with George W. Jackson, the bookseller, and it is to this gentleman that we owe the records still extant of the operation of the Panorama.[7] In January 1838, the frame rotunda, occupying Broadway at the corner of Mercer and Prince Streets, was completed; the cost, as given in Catherwood's account book was exactly $7,816.16. The Panorama's location was excellent; it fronted Billy Niblo's San Souci where the inebriated patrons could stumble over to the gas-lighted Panorama and be sobered by looking at a huge canvas of the Holy Land. An illustration of Catherwood's Panorama, only recently discovered, gives a graphic picture of the circular building, which thousands of New Yorkers visited in the years of its existence. It was the first and last permanent panorama in New York City, and the art critic of the *New-York Mirror* welcomed it with, 'We hail with no small interest the permanent establishment of panoramas in this city. Occasional exhibitions have met with more or less of the public attention, but we augur for the present a degree of patronage which shall do honour to our citizens.' [8] New Yorkers

---

* 'It was incredible,' writes P. A. Means in his *Newport Tower*, 'that a man like Catherwood whose later archaeological drawings are marvels of fidelity, could ever have perpetrated so false and misleading a picture as the interior view [of the Newport Tower engraved by Scholer].'

had seen their first panorama when 'Versailles,' painted by John Vanderlyn, a protégé of Aaron Burr, was shown, and there was an occasional exhibition by some journeyman artist. But Catherwood began the trend, and for more than a half a century panoramas were for millions of Americans their only formal entertainment. In 1847 John Banvard completed his Panorama of the Mississippi, 15,840 feet of continuous canvas exhibited on two upright revolving cylinders. After touring the Americas, Europe, and Asia, he reaped what was then, and is now, a fortune: $200,000. Commercially, the panorama had reached classical stature. A few years later another Panorama of the Mississippi was painted by I. J. Egan. It is important only in so far as it is the only known panoramic canvas to now exist in its entirety.*

The panoramic history in America began with Catherwood's 'Splendid Panorama of Jerusalem.' Advertisements inserted in all of the leading New York papers announced Jerusalem, 'a painting of the largest class, 10,000 square feet from drawings of Mr. Catherwood brilliantly illuminated every evening by upwards of 200 gas-lights—admission 25¢.' It had an excellent press; the *Mirror's* critic was fully impressed by the artist's background.

The establishment of Mr. Catherwood (a gentleman well known through the country for those admirable lectures on the 'land of the East' the result of many years of observant travelling) is on a scale equal to the successive production of a whole series of magnificent panoramic paintings, from original drawings—the most attractive of the whole host of London exhibitions.

The critic spoke of the 'high talent,' the 'truly brilliant artistical merit . . . Nothing can surpass,' he wrote, 'the style in which Jerusalem is brought before us.' He went into ecstasies over the 'architectural magnificence of the Mosque of Omar.' The Panorama had promised additional 'views'; as the *Mirror's* art critic

---

*In the collections of the University Museum, University of Pennsylvania, Philadelphia.[9]

Catherwood's Panorama. The only known illustration of New York's first Rotunda.

wrote, 'After this picture has remained long enough to satisfy the increasing curiosity of the publick, we are informed that pictures of Rome, of Lima, of Thebes . . . will succeed it. Truly this is noble work, and must, as in London, go on increasingly steady in popularity.' And so it did; Catherwood's account books exhibit rapidly rising daily receipts.

In the meantime his friend, John Lloyd Stephens, had written an excellent travel book *Incidents of Travel in Arabia Petraea . . . and the Holy Land.* It was published in 1837, and in the depths of Van Buren's depression had gone through twelve printings in a single year. In one of the later editions of the book when

49

Catherwood's Panorama was firmly established, Stephens propagandized it:

In justice to one who eminently deserves it. The author would endeavor to direct the attention of the public to MR. CATHERWOOD's PANORAMA OF JERUSALEM. Mr. Catherwood passed eight years in the East studying antiquities and architecture and making drawings of the ruined temples, monuments and cities of the Old World. The result of his labours is, that he has under his control, large panoramas of Jerusalem, Thebes, Damascus, Baalbec, Algiers, Carthage and Athens. Mr. Catherwood is connected with Burford, of the great Panoramas of Leicester Square, in London, and all his works are intended to succeed each other here and in that capital at regular intervals. He has commenced in this city with his Panorama of Jerusalem, and a large circular building covering an area of ten thousand square feet has been erected [The Rotunda at Prince and Broadway] for its exhibition. It was first exhibited at Burford's and so great was the sensation created in London that the first season it was visited by more than a hundred and forty thousand persons. It would be presumptious in the author to pronounce upon the work of a regularly-educated artist.*

The effect of this cumulative publicity was such that Catherwood decided to go to London and to purchase from Robert Burford additional panoramas, including copies of his own 'Thebes' and 'Baalbec.' He drew draft orders on Baring Brothers for $3,000 for the Niagara, Lima, and Thebes panoramas, drew an additional $250 for his passage to London and back, and arranged with George Jackson to pay 'Mrs. Catherwood twenty-two dollars a week.' [10] In November 1838 he left for London.

In a few months, Catherwood returned to America with several Burford panoramas. The rotunda soon offered 'Niagara' with 'Jerusalem,' then it was replaced by 'Thebes,' which was announced, 'as superior, as a work of art, to any Panorama ever

---

* Catherwood thought so highly of Stephens' preface that he had it printed on a broadside of the Panorama's Advertisement.

exhibited.' 'Mr. Catherwood' was on hand every evening at half past eight o'clock to lecture. The *Mirror's* critic gave a whole thoughtful column to The Panorama of Thebes, ending the piece with carefully weighed encomiums: 'Mr. Catherwood has made a good selection in the panorama of Thebes. It is beautifully painted. The perspective is equal to anything ever put upon canvas, and one can hardly rid himself of the idea that it is not nature that he is viewing.' [11] With this, his Panorama entered the realm of big business, and for the first time in his life Catherwood achieved something resembling financial success. The panoramas were then taken on the road, exhibited in Philadelphia, New Bedford, Providence, and Boston. It was in Boston, while the Panorama was in operation, that Catherwood exhibited part of his collection of five hundred watercolors, composed of work of the foremost artists of England—Turner, Stanfield, Prout, Harding, Boys, and Cattermole. One chatty critic wrote in dithyrambs about them, 'Of course you saw Catherwood's collection of water-coloured drawings now exhibiting here? They . . . are magnificent. Did you ever conceive the force of water-colouring before?' Catherwood then sold the entire collection at auction.[12]

Despite the pressing competition, Catherwood's panoramas remained the principal attraction in New York; Catlin's Indian Gallery was exhibiting down Broadway, as were the originals of Audubon's *Birds of America*; Niblo's Garden, directly across from the Rotunda, offered 'The Ravel Family on the TIGHT ROPE,' and later between beers 'REVOLVING STATUES.' The Apollo Gallery promised 'The Birth of Venus Beauty and Innocence Springing into Life,' and if one found all these dull, there was the 'Infernal Regions' at the City Saloon, 'Produced,' the advertisement read 'by the new Philosophical Apparatus, (lately from London) called the Nocturnal Polymorphous Fantascope.'

Yet Catherwood's panoramas still held the amusement spotlight.

Absorbing as all this success was to Catherwood, he had not lost his inner restlessness nor his passion for archaeological exploration, and the arrival of his old friend William Henry Bartlett in America for the second time served to remind him of their days together in the Levant. Bartlett, a pupil of John Britton, had met Catherwood in Jerusalem in 1833, and together they had walked through the fabled ruins of Transjordania. Bartlett had now been sent by his British publisher, George Virtue,[13] to America to collaborate with N. P. Willis on an illustrated *American Scenery*. And so in New York these old friends met again, and Catherwood was again aroused to exploration. And there were other reminders of the past; in July 1839 Lady Westmoreland, Catherwood's mistress in Rome, suddenly appeared in New York City; 'The Countess of Westmoreland,' announced the *Herald*, 'is sojourning at Waverly House which appears to suit her fine and fastidious taste. She tried the Carlton and left it, tried the Astor House and left it.' If Catherwood did not see the notice of her presence, for it was directly opposite his own Panorama advertisement, it was because new events were shaping themselves, events that would change his destiny. He was, with John Lloyd Stephens, completing plans for an expedition into strife-torn Central America to search out the ruins of mysterious lost civilizations.

Chapter Six

THE MAYAN DISCOVERIES
IN CENTRAL AMERICA

1 : COPÁN

In the autumn of 1839, after three years of gestation, the expedition to Central America and the Mayas was born, born out of the curiosity of Catherwood and the enthusiasm of John Lloyd Stephens. When these two had first met in London, in 1836, they had discussed the rumors that were welling up out of Central America of stone cities and temples buried behind the green curtain of the jungles. Up to that moment only three books [1] had been published on these ruins of tropical America—publications shadowy in evidence and exaggerated in illustration. These were mainly on a single site, called Palenque, a mysterious city entangled in the forests of the Mexican province of Chiapas. These ruins, variously ascribed to Egyptians, Phoenicians, and—most accepted by the antiquarians—the wandering Tribes of Israel, completely fascinated Catherwood. For he had studied almost all of the ancient cultures of the Near East and knew that, as imperfect as were the illustrations in these books, the civilizations they depicted were not seemingly derived from the Old World. Although Stephens and Catherwood in 1836 agreed to take a future journey together, Central America, apparently, was not specifically mentioned. It was only when they were again in America, after Catherwood had

53

achieved his first real success with his panoramas, and Stephens a certain financial independence with his two published books of travels, that their conversations turned again to these mysterious ruins.

In 1838, another book on these ruins appeared. It was written by that fantastic *voyageur* Count Waldeck [2] and published in Paris. This handsome folio with hand-colored lithographs brought a new name into the antiquarian vocabulary—Uxmal. This ruin, drawn in Waldeck's best French manner, finished and elegant, was located in Yucatán. The Waldeck volume had been brought to America by the Astor House Book Shop, the owners of which, as specialists in antiquarian literature, invited the discoverers-to-be of the Mayan civilization to the store; they spent much of their time thumbing over the newly arrived books and there they saw the Waldeck. Once again Catherwood's suspicion was aroused in regard to the character of this culture, for Waldeck had drawn pyramids in the Egyptian style decorated with statues in the full round that were in all reality Roman in feeling. Waldeck and his American researches had become highly suspect, and not alone to Catherwood.* What we do know, and with certainty, about the genesis of this Central American expedition that resulted in the archaeological discoveries comes from the journal of John Russell Bartlett,[3] who wrote:

I claim to have first suggested it to Mr. Stephens. . . One day in my office I said to [him] 'Why do you not undertake the exploration of Yucatán and Central America.' . . I invited him to come to my house when I would show him Waldeck's work on Yucatán, a

---

* William Prescott, then writing his *Conquest of Mexico*, wrote to Fanny Calderón de la Barca, 'I have a very beautiful work, containing coloured drawings of the ruins in Yucatán . . . by Waldeck, whose history you probably know. Now I really am afraid to rely on them [the illustrations] Waldeck talks so big, and so dogmatically, and I don't know, now that I have a *soupçon* . . . he is a good deal of a charlatan. And I should not like to be led into blunders by a confidence in him. Will you be so good in your next to let me know whether I am right, that is whether sensible persons in Mexico place confidence in him. . .'
5 December 1840.

beautiful work in folio, containing views of some of the ruined edifices in that country, which I had imported a short time previous from Paris.

For the next weeks John Lloyd Stephens was completely absorbed in puzzling out this civilization and speculating on its origin. There were nightly conferences with Catherwood. The Bartlett journal continues:

Fortunately, for Stephens, Mr. Frederick Catherwood, a distinguished architect and draughtsman who had spent much time in Egypt and the Holy Land and with whom he was on intimate terms, was then in New York. Mr. Catherwood had great enthusiasm in everything appertaining to architecture and was an ardent lover of the picturesque and of archaeological researches. Mr. Stephens made him a favourable offer to accompany him to Central America which offer he at once accepted.

Catherwood then turned his Panorama over to George Jackson, the bookseller, and his partner, purchased the necessary equipment, and on 3 October 1839 sailed with Stephens to British Honduras on the brig *Mary Ann*.

Catherwood always had the misfortune of carrying on his explorations in war's cauldron; when he toured Hellas, Greeks and Turks waged a war over his head, even as he was working at the Parthenon; in Syria, Pasha and Sheik scourged the earth about him; and in Egypt, the highly tempered Mehemet Ali waged ceaseless war on his opposition. America brought no surcease of war in Catherwood's career. After landing at Belize in British Honduras and making their way up the río Dulce into Lake Izabal, on the old side-wheeler *Vera Paz*, they found themselves in Guatemala—Guatemala in a state of revolution. Back of those vividly green jungle walls, war waged, unchecked by compromise; the five Central American States, Guatemala, Honduras, Costa Rica, Nicaragua, and Salvador, were engaged in a three-cornered struggle. The official at the lake port of Izabal very much doubted if

Stephens' diplomatic passport would fully protect them. They secured guides, pack-mules, and made plans to cross, in the first days of November, the Mico Mountain range. This was to lead them through the jungle into the interior country.

The Mico route was the only entrance to interior Guatemala, a jungle trail fetlock deep of mud and gloomed by immense, parasite-covered trees. It was not precisely madness that took Stephens from a profitable law profession and Catherwood from his Panorama into the mysterious Central American jungles in search for ruins; but if it was not madness then it was probably the next thing to it; a fevered enthusiasm for archaeology and the search for the unknown. Catherwood, then forty years old, must have often questioned this enthusiasm as he guided his mule over fallen trees and extricated himself from mud holes; probably this questioning reached its climax when he was thrown from his mule and struck his head against the exposed roots of a tree. From the depths of the mud where his head was partly buried 'he broke,' wrote Stephens, 'the awful silence to utter an exclamation which seemed to come from the bottom of his heart that if he had known of this mountain, I might have come to Central America alone.'

On the second day they emerged from the jungle into pine savannahs and stands of tall, spine-armed cactus. They passed through the villages of El Pozo, Encuentros, and Gualán, each village a cluster of houses of sun-dried bricks and red-tiled roofs. Upon entering the larger village of Chiquimula they found a thousand soldiers lined up for parade; now they knew they were in the vortex of revolution. Here they turned their path southward into Honduras to a place called Copán. Although Stephens' diplomatic instructions read that he should proceed to Guatemala City at once, search out the seat of government, and present his credentials in order to carry forward the next step of his diplomatic itinerary, he had ideas of his own. Before leaving New York he had read a short article 'A Description of the Ruins of Copán' by Colonel Juan Galindo,[4] which brought into archaeological vocabulary three names of ruined sites, Uxmal, Palenque, and Copán. Galindo, actually an Irishman whose name other than this *nom de guerre* we do not know, was holding office as Governor of El Peten in Guatemala. An intelligent man, Colonel Galindo; having threaded his way through the labyrinths of legend and apparently read an earlier Spanish account of the ruins of Copán which had never been published, he personally explored the site. He wrote a short, accurate paper on the ruins, which he published in North America; and so Copán was selected by Stephens and Catherwood, although it appeared on no map as easily accessible. Copán was to mark the genesis of American archaeology.

The archaeological explorers followed the south road to Copán over the unmarked frontier of Guatemala into Honduras, where, as befitted the nature of the violent land, they were arrested. In the little village of Comatán, where a tall white-painted church with baroque corkscrew-shaped columns dominated clusters of small houses of sun-dried brick, the explorers were set upon by a retinue of comic-opera soldiers followed by a tableau of Indians who enacted a scene which, had it not had elements of great personal danger, would have been one of Stephens' amusing 'incidents of travel.' Released forty-eight hours later, after Frederick Catherwood had made a learned discourse on the laws of nations—which little moved their captors—they continued until they arrived at a jungle-covered valley; this, at 3,000 feet altitude, was the ancient site of the Mayan city of Copán.

The seventeenth of November 1839 remains a notable date in American archaeological history, for on that day Frederick Catherwood set up his camera lucida in the jungle-bound ruins and began the first real limning of Mayan art. Words cannot recreate the awesome wonder that John Lloyd Stephens and Frederick Catherwood experienced when they looked upon the Acropolis of Copán. Covered with trees that spread slow ruin with their

57

pallid roots, draped with wrist-thick lianas that wound the beautiful stone-carvings in woody embrace, tenanted only by sad-faced monkeys, here were the remains of what was once a great religious center. One glance at the sculptured stones and they knew that the people who had built this city had been nurtured by some great culture. Catherwood, who had explored, at one time or another, every known Old-World civilization possessed the touchstone of archaeological experience. And he did not hesitate to apply it. Whatever the name or origin of the people who had constructed this city, they were, aesthetically, as advanced as the Egyptians. If Copán really existed, then Palenque and Uxmal might also; and since these cities lay hundreds of miles apart on the periphery of Central America, then the jungle between them probably contained other buried sites of ruined cities. They had found not mere ruin, but the promise of an entire lost civilization.

After some difficulty with the native population, dissipated by the fifty dollars that Stephens paid for the Copán site, they began the work of clearing the vegetation in order that Catherwood might begin his surveys. First the ancient Mayan site was measured, and from the figures Catherwood fashioned a most creditable map—considering the morass of jungle—although in its printing, the cardinal points were reversed 180°, the map's north becoming south in the engraving. This survey revealed an artificial acropolis built out of valley floor, forming itself into five large plazas and two principal courtyards dominated by three truncated pyramids. Extending out from the main acropolis was the Great Plaza, 800 feet long, theatered by tiers of stone seats. Here, in times past, Mayas dressed in barbaric magnificence witnessed the exhibition of pageantry that marked the ritual-enlivened life of the people. The cutting of stone from the neighboring cliffs, the rolling of these huge thirty-ton monoliths on wooden rollers and the raising, polishing, and decoration of the religious center was an immense human achievement. The explorers were unable to

58

clear the pyramids, in the time allotted to them, of the centuries of detritus, and so finding not enough of architecture to make judgment, Catherwood gave most of his attention to the upright stone monoliths, intricately carved and painted steles that dominated the Great Plaza.[5] The huge stone figures were dressed in the trappings of Mayan priests—open mouthed and staring—and along the sides of the steles coursed mysteriously unintelligible glyphs. Catherwood instantly recognized the fundamental aesthetic difference between the Mayan and Egyptian glyphs, for the Egyptians had treated their hieroglyphs as a mere picture; these glyphs were unlike anything that Catherwood had ever seen. He was amazed, as was his countryman Aldous Huxley, a century later, at the ease with which the sculptors had used their neolithic tools. The Mayan craftsmen at Copán had, as Huxley wrote, 'treated their twenty-two foot monoliths as a Chinese craftsman might treat a piece of ivory.'

Yet before mastering the intricacies of Mayan art, Catherwood had his troubles. Stephens wrote:

After several hours absence, I returned to Mr. Catherwood, and reported upwards of fifty objects to be copied. I found him not so well pleased as I expected. He was standing with his feet in the mud, and was drawing with his gloves on to protect his hands from the *moschetoes*. As we feared, the designs were so intricate and complicated, the subjects so entirely new and unintelligible, that he had great difficulty in drawing. He had made several attempts, both with the camera lucida and without, but failed to satisfy himself or even me, who was less severe in criticism. The 'Idol' seemed to defy his art.[6]

Frederick Catherwood at first found the Mayan art form beyond his immediate comprehension. This strange art lay outside of the Indo-European traditions. Its tropical luxuriance of detail seemed to absorb the theme of the sculpture, for the Maya, working in an involved style dictated by a ritualistic religion and an

59

elaborate symbolism, had developed it out of the stream of aesthetic history. Mayan art, like all of pre-Columbian American art, had flowered in isolation. It had had no contact with the historical evolution of art that formed, for thousands of years, the background of all of man's art expression, for, as Pál Keleman writes,

The fabric of Old World archaeology and art history is like a vast web stretching from the Roman ramparts of England to the delicately drawn woodcuts of Japan, from the Byzantine icons of the Russian Steppes to the wondrous world of the royal tombs of Egypt. . . Yet, remote as certain points lie from one another, as different as are the styles which they produced; nevertheless, it is clear that details and even whole ideas are incorporated, adapted and developed inter-regionally. At the time Greek art began to flourish, about 500 B.C., there were nearly three thousand years of cultural heritage from which to draw inspiration.[7]

Mayan art, then, was the 'purest' of art, maturing in the splendid isolation of a continent of vast and complex geography. For man, as 'animal,' it need hardly be repeated, did not originate in America, but made his entry—at least all known physical evidence points to it—over the land bridge of the Bering Strait some hundreds of centuries ago. Thus, while man as 'animal' did not evolve in America, man, as 'culture bearer' did, and this native art, passing through a long period of development, reached its cultural climax in the densely populated regions of Central America and Mexico. However, the three divisions of cultural anthropology, the ages of stone, bronze, and iron—first distinguished in 1832 by Christian Jurgen Thomsen of Copenhagen—are not applicable to the Mayas, for they never left the neolithic plane of human culture: the carving of stone was done by stone. Metal, when it came to the tropical-American cultures, arrived late, not much before the eleventh century, and by that time the Old Empire of the Maya had already disappeared. While the Andean cultures of

South America perfected bronze tools, the stone celt remained the instrument of the Mayan sculpture mason; Copán, which Catherwood and Stephens had rediscovered after a thousand years of oblivion, was, like all the other religious centers of the Mayas which they would visit, carved of stone by stone.

Frederick Catherwood was unaware that Copán, built during the 'Old Empire' period, marked the extreme southern expansion of the Mayas; when its structures were erected, the culture of the Maya was already matured. Centuries before the building of Copán, the Mayas (whose precise geographical genesis is not known, but deduced to have been the Huasteca region in Mexico) had, by casual wanderings that extended over centuries, infiltered through the jungle-bound highlands of Guatemala into Honduras, into Mexico, and into the forested section of the flat Yucatán peninsula. Between the first and ninth centuries of the Christian era—the extreme dates of the period of 'Old Empire' [8]—religious centers mushroomed out of the jungle, all built by the incredible labor of the Indians, who raised white sculptured towers until they rose above the forest.

The political basis of this American culture seemingly was theocratic communism. Its economy based on corn revolved around the agricultural milpa; maize, beans, and squash were cultivated in such quantities as to provide leisure. Given no immediate competitors, for there is no evidence of any other advanced civilization having occupied the area before the Mayas, given a beneficent climate, a productive earth, it allowed a native feeling for texture and for creation and caused the birth of a culture. Out of the void they created in nine centuries innumerable magnificent religious centers. 'A people,' wrote Elie Faure, 'is like a man. When he has disappeared, nothing is left of him unless he has taken the precaution to leave his imprint on the stones of the road.' One of the most spectacular of these 'imprints' was the ruins of Copán.

Half a century would pass before archaeologists, led to the

ruins by the facile pen of Stephens and the equally facile brush of Catherwood, would determine how and under what circumstance the Mayan sculptors of Copán erected these immense monolithic portraits. For, obsessed with time, the Mayan priests had their sculptors carve elaborate calendars on the sides and back of the steles, and these marked the time of their erection. For 365 years at Copán, in intervals of twenty-, ten-, and five-year periods, these 'dated' monuments were erected. Then, without warning, they stop, the great city of Copán gradually is deserted, and within a century it is reclaimed by the jungle. And there it remained in oblivion for a thousand years until 17 November 1839, when Catherwood and Stephens began the first systematic investigations of the Maya.

Catherwood worked stubbornly through rain, rubble, and revolution to unravel the Mayan designs. An artist who had made casts of the Greek sculptures while a revolution whirled about his head was not going to be put off by the first difficulties. We have no portrait, no word description of 'Mr. Catherwood,' but Catherwood, standing in pools of water, his hands gloved to keep off the *moschetoes,* putting down on paper in sepia the first authentic drawings of the Mayan monuments, needs little other portraiture; obstinacy and enthusiasm are the touchstones of his character.

After thirteen days at Copán, John Lloyd Stephens' diplomatic duties made it necessary that he leave for Guatemala to search out the Central Government and present his credentials. Catherwood was left alone at Copán to finish the work of copying the principal sculptures. There he remained a month, refusing to yield to either annoying mestizos or mosquitoes. No record exists of the number of drawings he completed. In Stephens' book in the Copán section there are twenty-three engravings and five woodcuts, yet these are, it is believed, only a fraction of what he accomplished. His sepia drawings, Piranesi-like, in taut emotion, developed the dramatic overtones of this primitive art. Yet it did not affect his fidelity; the late Dr. Sylvanus G. Morley, Maya scholar, writes of those drawings:

Catherwood's portrayal [of Stele B] is accurate and conveys a forceful idea of the original. He has faithfully rendered the expression of serenity and dignity, so characteristic of the faces of the Copán stelae and his delineation of the back of Stela F . . . shows painstaking care. Similarly, his drawing of the back of Stela F . . . is so accurate that it is possible to decipher the date inscribed from it. . .

. . . When it is taken into consideration that the Maya hieroglyphic writing was a sealed book at the time he visited Copán, and that he knew nothing about the subject matter of the glyphs he drew, such accuracy is remarkable.[9]

The tribute from his countryman, Alfred P. Maudslay, who followed him to Copán, forty-five years later, and who did the first excavations of this Maya city-state, gives no less an encomium: 'It is to the charming pages of Stephens and the beautiful drawings of Catherwood that the world in general is indebted for the knowledge of the wonders of Copán.'[10]

There are limitations to an art spirit, even as pertinacious and indomitable a spirit as Catherwood's. His body bitten by mosquitoes, his blood filled with the plasmodia of malaria, his toes full of chiggers, assaulted by man and climate, he found it no longer bearable, and so, three weeks after Stephens' departure, he too left Copán for Guatemala. Alone on the trail, he was robbed and deserted by his servant, even while his body boiled with the satanic heat of malarial fever. Yet when he came to the río Motagua and heard that there were other ruins buried in the forest that surrounded a place called Quiriguá, he threw aside his ague and went off in search of more ruins.*

---

* Catherwood later returned to Copán, bearing a passport made out by Stephens indicating that he was the 'Secretary of the Legation.' 'I sent Mr. Catherwood,' explains Stephens to the American Secretary of State, 'a separate

2 : QUIRIGUÁ

North of the río Motagua, a river that makes a deep cicatrix of the Guatemalan earth on its way to the sea, are the misty outlines of mountains called the Sierra del Mico; below it was a village of twenty palm-thatched houses and a larger house, the home of the *hacendado*, who possessed a cattle ranch of some dimensions; six miles northeast of it was the site of the ruins of Quiriguá. Catherwood, who made his way toward it, had heard first of the ruins from a Jamaica Englishman living at the hacienda, a Mr. Meiney, known throughout the area as Don Carlos Meiney.

In January 1840, Frederick Catherwood discovered the ruins of Quiriguá. Enveloped completely by a thick jungle, Quiriguá stood about three-quarters of a mile from the left bank of the río Motagua. There Catherwood found mounds, oblong and square, varying from six to forty feet in height, faced with sculptured stone; humus of the jungle had enveloped it. The archaeological treasures of Quiriguá, however, were thirteen superbly carved monolithic steles, only two of which were then visible. One glance at these huge monoliths and Catherwood knew, as Stephens wrote, that 'The general character of these ruins is the same as Copán.' This deduction was most accurate, for Quiriguá *had* been a colony of Copán. Copán in Honduras was one of the large centers of the Mayan 'Old Empire.' It had remarkably increased in population owing to the successful conquest of nature by the Mayan agricultural system, but the ceaseless burning and planting without the addition of fertilizer or crop rotation stunted each successive planting, until it became no longer economically feasible to replant. The milpas were then abandoned and colonies set up. Quiriguá was such a colony of Copán, enduring, so far as

passport as Secretary of the Legation. . . It is not a perfect protection but it is of very great value. I trust that if it is an assumption you will excuse it, in consideration of the advantages it gives me in the objects I proposed to myself in coming in to this country. . .'

its dated monuments are a record, for 65 years, between *c.* 746–810. Immigrants from Copán found near the site of the proposed city, a range of hills of exposed sandstone. After the colony was set up, the Indian sculptors quarried solid sandstone shafts, and these were rolled over the jungle floor to the established religious center at Quiriguá. The Mayas, now beyond the experimental phase of neolithic culture, raised and carved the first stele at Quiriguá. It was dated in Christian correlation probably about A.D. 746.

These Catherwood discovered, and even though he was still suffering from the alternating chills and fever brought on by the malarial parasites he set up his easel and sketchily copied two of the monoliths: [11] these, published in Stephens' book in 1841, became the first notice of these ruins; Catherwood then left for Guatemala City.

On Christmas night of 1839, just when Stephens was about to leave to go to the Plaza de Toros, there was a loud knock at the door, 'and in rode Mr. Catherwood, armed to the teeth,' wrote Stephens, 'pale and thin, most happy at reaching Guatemala, but not half so happy as I was to see him. He was in advance of his luggage, but I dressed him and carried him immediately to the Plaza de Toros.' Though the soldiery of Rafael Carrera was terrifying the whole countryside, Catherwood took to the convent at Ciudad Vieja in company with the famous and garrulous Padre Alcantara ('Intelligent, educated and energetic'), while Stephens, on his diplomatic mission, set off alone to find the Government of Central America.

In April 1840, Stephens having returned without success in finding a Central Government to which to present his credentials, they made ready their plans for the thousand-mile expedition into Mexico and to the ruins of Palenque. They were momentarily deterred by the information that two Englishmen were recently killed while trying to reach the same place. Lieutenant Nichols, aide-de-camp to Colonel McDonald of British Honduras, told them that Mr. Patrick Walker, Secretary of the Colonial Government, with Captain John Herbert Caddy of the British Royal Artillery,[12] whom they had known in Belize, had been 'speared by the Indians.' This did not halt them. Stephens gained an audience with Rafael Carrera, dictator since he had defeated his arch rival General Francisco Morazán; and from him they obtained papers of identification. They climbed to the pine regions of Los Altos, skirted the lovely Lago Atitlán several thousand feet above sea level, passed the Indian town of Solalá, a Cachiquel market center, moved southward to Quetzaltenango, 'the place of the quetzal,' and there ran into Carrera's soldiers, bloodstained and fierce-eyed, returning from their massacres. Along the way they picked up another companion, an American named Henry Pawling who had managed in Guatemala a cochineal plantation. He had excellent command of Spanish, was well-armed, and knew the country. Stephens added the young black-bearded Pawling to the expedition and they continued riding northeast, through towering cliffs and yawning chasms, to the Mexican-Guatemalan frontier. Somewhere along this trail occurred a curious incident, which gave rise to an amazing tale told to Mrs. L. E. Elliot-Joyce,[13] by Dr. Alfred P. Maudslay, the British explorer of the Mayan ruins, who followed chronologically his countryman, Catherwood.

When on their way through northern Guatemala in 1840 it happened that Catherwood dismounted at a difficult mountain road, rubbed among the rocks and found some rather remarkable fragments. As he examined them, Stephens called to him to hurry; Catherwood put the bits of stone in his pocket, and eventually in his baggage, without thinking any more of them or the place whence he had taken them until he reached New York. There he showed them to friends and they reached the hands of an essayer, who pronounced them to be wonderfully extraordinarily rich specimens of gold-bearing ore.

Catherwood told the tale to a British diplomat,[14] newly accredited (and about to set out for Guatemala), and this gentleman, becoming friendly with Rafael Carrera, repeated it to the Indian dictator. Carrera wanted money badly, and he saw chances of enormous wealth to carry out all his plans. Greatly excited, he begged the Minister to offer every inducement to Catherwood including a share in the mine, if he would come to Guatemala and identify the spot. Catherwood accepted the proposition, bought machinery and camping equipment, saw it shipped in a schooner from New Orleans, and decided not to accompany it but to take passage in a steamer, a new venture, about to make her trial trip from the mouth of the Mississippi to the Caribbean waters. The steamer set out; but she never reached port. Nor was any person on board ever heard of again.

When at last the vessel had to be given up, when Carrera realized that Catherwood had perished and with Catherwood all hopes of finding the gold mine, his grief and disappointment knew no bounds; he literally tore his hair. Also he ordered searches to be made in the locality of the find, so far as it could be identified from Catherwood's own casual remembrance. For he with no map of the country had had no idea of the position of the place, but said that he could recognize it again.

For months, bodies of men, sent by Carrera, scoured the mountain paths taking scraps of rock from every cliff and boulder in likely and unlikely regions, urged desperately by the President. But never did they find poor Catherwood's mine and from that day to this no sign of it has been discovered. This tale was told to me by the explorer of Guatemalan ruins, Dr. Alfred P. Maudslay, who had it from the diplomat.

Catherwood, of course, did not perish in the Caribbean. How really obscure he was is revealed by the fact that Dr. Maudslay, who followed in Catherwood's wake among the Mayas, did not know that he died in the sinking of the *S.S. Arctic*, and that Mrs. Joyce, the wife of the well-informed Curator of American Archaeology in the British Museum, accepted the account as true.

3 : PALENQUE

In the first week of May 1840, they came upon the ruins of Palenque, the mysterious stone city buried in the jungle, of which they had heard so much. Palenque, which was eight miles from a post-village from which it had derived its name, lay high on the escarpments of a jungle-covered mountain overlooking a flat river-filled savannah. In the blue haze of distance was the Caribbean Sea. After much bickering with the local gentry, who tried to discourage them from visiting the ruins, the explorers set out at daybreak, climbed the sisyphus-trails, and arrived at the famous Palenque. In a chaos of vegetation they discovered a triple-courted building called El Palacio, whose stuccoed façade still exhibited parts of its brilliant decoration, and other temples and structures bearing high roof combs on which the Indians had lavished their artistry. The whole site, although on the edge of a mountain, had been terraced and joined together in its heyday by stone roads. A river, the Otolum, which flowed through the site, had been directed into the stone culvert.

Constructed sometime during the end of the Mayan Old Empire, its earliest monument is dated *c.* A.D. 642 *—'Palenque demonstrates,' writes Pál Kelemen, 'that the Maya had a broad and elastic architectural conception which they adapted to local conditions and topography, never allowing it to become crystallized into stereotyped patterns that limited their artistic activity.' [15] The research began with a clearing away of the roots and lianas that ceaselessly sapped the stone work. A general map was made of the ruins and a detailed plan of the Palacio, and then an architectural analysis of the structure. For the first time Catherwood was given some idea of the Mayas' architectural techniques; he noticed instantly that the Mayas had no concept of the true arch, which he remembered was also a limitation of other archaic cultures. It became immediately apparent to him that these American builders, like the primitive Egyptians and Greeks did not know

---

* The dates given here are based on the correlation of Maya and Christian chronologies according to the Goodman-Martinez-Hernandez-Thompson Correlation Formula, expanded by Dr. S. G. Morley in *The Ancient Maya*, 1946.

the principle of the true arch. Here his architect's eyes saw that the 'arch' stones were cut to special shapes, so that gravity could hold them in position. They were laid layer on layer until they met overhead. The roof was heavily weighted to hold this corbeled arch, giving the Maya structures a high entablature. This was put to extensive and varied use. On it the Maya craftsmen molded strikingly beautiful sculptured stucco ornaments—parts of it retained the color even after a thousand years of decay. The Mayas knew nothing, apparently, of bonding corners; they lacked knowledge of the formula by which to lay off a right angle, but the entire concept of the structure was barbarically beautiful and, considering that theirs was a neolithic culture, it was worthy to stand with the great architectures of the world.

Of the builders of this culture, Stephens and Catherwood knew nothing. They had no name and at the time no written history. All the documents that the earlier Spanish historiographers had prepared on this civilization still lay buried in official Spanish archives. The only guide to its history were the hundreds of glyphs that decorated the interiors of its fetid walls. One thing, however, they discovered at once. Although Palenque in Mexico was separated from Copán in Honduras by 300 air-miles—a geographical void of jungle, swamp, mountain, and chasm—the two mysterious sites had been built by the same people, the same culture. This could be discerned not only in the stylistic sequences of their art but in their glyphic writing as well. 'The hieroglyphics,' wrote Stephens,[16] 'are the same as we found at Copán and Quiriguá. The intermediate country is now occupied by races of Indians speaking many different languages and entirely unintelligible to each other, but there is room for belief that the whole of this country was once occupied by the same race, speaking the same language, or at least having the same written characters.' Without fully knowing it, Catherwood and Stephens had described, geographically, the Mayan Old Empire. Extending from the highlands of Chiapas to the valley of Copán, in the moist as well as the dry regions of Middle America, the Old Empire survived for almost four hundred years. Palenque, the most northern, Tikal, Uaxactun, Piedras Negras, Naranjo in Central Guatemala, and Copán and its chief satellite, Quiriguá, the most southern, were the Old Empire's chief population centers.

Catherwood, after several false starts, began to draw the stucco figures. He passed from these into the dark dank interior of the Temple of the Cross, where he discovered an immense stone entablature composed of two full-sized figures carved in bas-relief offering a grotesque mannikin to the image of the deified quetzal bird. Despite its complicated design, its tropical luxuriance of detail, the row upon row of hieroglyphics, Catherwood drew it with his usual fidelity. There were two such entablatures to copy, and amid the flood of insects and rain Catherwood stuck painfully to his work.

In the thirty-five days that they spent at Palenque, Catherwood completed upwards of fifty sepia drawings and, as a part of the scientific survey, a map. But he had suffered as a result of all this activity: insects bit at his hands and face, niguas, sand-fleas bored into his toes until he was hardly able to stand. The food was monotonous and dull and, moreover, scarce. When Stephens went down to the village of Santo Domingo de Palenque to remedy the food problem he was forced to remain for several days before he had assembled enough to be worthy of a return trip to the ruins. When he did return to Palenque he was startled by the change: 'Mr. Catherwood's appearance startled me. He was wan and gaunt; lame, like me, from the bites of insects; his face was swollen and his left arm hung with rheumatism, as if paralyzed.'

The rainy season, too, fell full upon them in the last days of May, the hurricanes sweeping in from the Gulf of Yucatán tore at the trees, sent branches crashing about the ruins, 'but,' Stephens writes, 'we remained until Mr. Catherwood had finished his last drawing; and on Saturday, the first of June, like rats leaving a sinking ship, we broke up and left the ruins.'

At the village of Santo Domingo de Palenque they rested for a few days, while Catherwood gained strength. Yet despite his advanced state of collapse, he observed two small Indians whose profiles very much resembled those that he had seen on the ancient walls of Palenque. He started to draw them, but they, unwilling and shy, refused to return. This incident was seized upon by P. T. Barnum a few years later when he exhibited in New York two Indian children, whom he referred to as 'Aztec Lilliputians.' Stephens had given some credence to a story by the Padre of Santa Cruz de Quiché about a mysterious Mayan city, buried in the mountains of the Quiché country, beyond the reach of trails, and Barnum ingeniously combined the two elements and said that the Aztec Lilliputians had come from this unexplored city. These exhibits were accompanied by a curious and rare pamphlet that used the illustrations of Catherwood to authenticate presumably these Lilliputian marvels. Later Catherwod, with unwonted warmth, wrote, 'The story told of their capture in the published account of them, it is scarcely worth while to refute, and I will only say that, in my opinion, it has not even the semblance of truth.' [17]

The Maya explorers left Santo Domingo de Palenque, reached the río Usumacinta, and began their descent to the sea. 'From Mr. Catherwood's condition' wrote Stephens, 'I had fear that we should not be able to accomplish what we proposed.' They went down by canoe to the Laguna del Terminos and reached the town of Laguna. On the Island of Carmen, through the kindness of Mr. Charles Russell, American Consul, a ship was found to take them 120 miles to the port of Sisal, which was the port of entry to Mérida, capital of Yucatán. Henry Pawling, who had been instructed by Catherwood, was left behind to return to Palenque in order to make casts of the Mayan sculptures.

Having arrived in Mérida they pushed on to the ruins of Uxmal, which lay fifty miles south of the capital. After a journey through the scrub-jungles of Yucatán, the malignant fever was again upon Catherwood and he rested in his hammock within the hacienda of Don Simón Peón, which bordered the ruins. Stephens went out alone to Uxmal. Later in the day he broke in breathlessly upon the fevered Catherwood and reported he had seen a large open field with mounds, ruins, vast buildings, and grand terraces in good preservation and in picturesque effect almost equal to the ruins of Thebes. 'Such was the report I made to Mr. Catherwood on my return, who, lying in his hammock, unwell and out of spirits, told me that I was romancing; but early the next morning we were on the ground.'

They made elaborate plans, but to no avail. Catherwood was deathly ill. At Uxmal, in front of the long, intricately-carved façade of the 'Governor's Palace,' Frederick Catherwood, Maya artist, collapsed.

'As I followed Mr. Catherwood through the woods,' remembered Stephens, 'borne on the shoulders of Indians, the stillness broken only by the shuffle of the Indians' feet, and under my great apprehensions for his health, it seemed almost as if I were following his bier.' [18]

They sailed for the United States and reached New York on 31 July 1840.

4 : INCIDENTS OF TRAVEL IN CENTRAL AMERICA

John Lloyd Stephens as soon as he returned began the writing of the book that was to become a monument in American archaeological history. Catherwood started to work on its illustrations. Harper & Brothers, who had so successfully published Stephens' two previous books, allowed them to understand that no expense would be spared to make it one of the finest books ever published in America, as indeed it was so characterized by Edgar Allan Poe, who later reviewed it.* Catherwood, working closely with Stephens, was given entire charge of the illustrations and the designing of the proposed two volumes. Catherwood chose six well-known New York engravers: Stephen Henry Gimber (illustrator of Stephens' first book); Dr. Alexander Anderson, who executed the wood-engraving vignettes; Archibald L. Dick, the engraver of Henry Inman; John Halpin, one of Harper's engravers; and finally Jordan and Lossing. Catherwood had to see that the engravings closely followed his own sepia and watercolor drawings and that the hieroglyphics were faithfully copied. Unfortunately, the engravings were hurriedly done and Catherwood's original designs suffered greatly. He also designed the cover of the book so that the sides would be stamped with the design of the Sun-God from the Temple of the Sun at Palenque, and on the back of the binding coursed hieroglyphics taken from the Temple of Inscriptions. In September 1841, *Incidents of Travel in Central America, Chiapas, and Yucatán*, with its eighty engravings and at the extraordinarily high price of five dollars, made its appearance. It had immediate acclaim and went through ten printings in three months. The reviews were excellent in America as well as in London, where it quickly made its appearance. The book brought Stephens and Catherwood to the attention of William H. Prescott, who was then writing the *Conquest of Mexico*. 'You have made a tour,' Prescott wrote to Stephens, 'over a most interesting ground, the very forum of American ruins.' [19] To Fanny Calderón de la Barca,[20] the spirited Scotch schoolmistress who married a Spanish ambassador, Prescott wrote, 'I suppose you have hardly seen

---

* 'The work [*Incidents of Travel in Central America*] is certainly a magnificent one—perhaps the most interesting book of travel ever published.' Poe writing in *Grahams Magazine*, October 1841.

Stephens' work yet . . . the narrative is spirited. *But the real value of the work lies in the drawings* and the simple description of the ruins.' And later, '. . . Too much praise cannot be given to Mr. Catherwood's drawings in this connection. They carry with them a perfect assurance of his fidelity, in this, how different from his predecessors, who have never failed by some over-finish or by their touches for effect to throw an air of improbability, or at best, uncertainty, over the whole.'

Catherwood's drawings at first were questioned by Baron Friederichsthal, who went to Yucatán after Stephens' return, carrying his letter of introduction to Mérida. This criticism caused a mild controversy,[21] but a century of exploration has confirmed the accuracy of Frederick Catherwood's pioneer work among the Mayas.

Chapter Seven

THE MAYAS OF YUCATÁN

1 : UXMAL

In the autumn of 1841, having decided to return for another expedition to Central America, Stephens and Catherwood, accompanied by a third member, Dr. Samuel Cabot Jr.,[1] of Boston,
readied their equipment and in considerable secrecy sailed to
Yucatán.

The archaeological researches of the second expedition were
to be confined wholly within the realm of what has been termed
the Mayan New Empire. Catherwood, although he observed the
more highly stylized decorations and suspected some architectural-
cultural change because of some cultural evolution, did not know
then, as we do now, that Yucatán, between the seventh and fif-
teenth centuries, housed a Mayan civilization that had undergone
considerable change. The end of the ninth century brought more
or less to a close what had been the center of the Old Empire—the
wet-zone culture of such places as Copán, Uaxactun, Tikal,
Palenque, and the other cultural constellations of the Old Empire.
The center of Mayan culture now shifted to the dry-zone area,
Northern Yucatán, where the final drama, the conquest by the
Toltec and Spaniard, was to take place.

The disintegration of the Maya Empire had begun somewhere in the seventh century from a cause or causes not fully

75

explained. Whether it was an abandonment of the region because
of an interpretation of an evil augury by their priests—scarcely
credible—or disease (much doubted, since the migration was
casual and extended over a long period), or conquest by other
tribes which is also an improbable explanation, since the deserted
cities show only time's decay, not war's rapine, we are not able
to say. Climatic change is another consideration that has its logic,
but probably the best explanation is gradual disintegration of the
society owing to their ruinous agricultural practices. Frankly we
do not know. What is known as certain is that from the tenth
century until the coming of the Spaniards, the Mayas were con-
centrated in the northern part of Yucatán. Still they did not live in
isolated grandeur; they were part of a general cultural pattern.
In central Mexico there were the Toltecs. They had been establishing trading colonies for many centuries. In the eleventh century
the Toltecs invaded Yucatán. The cult of Quetzalcoatl took possession of the Mayas and began among other things to influence
their architecture. The Feathered Serpent, the open-mouthed, fang-
displaying snake, whose scales are elongated into the green plumes
of the quetzal (an excellent symbol of evolution), became the
principal decorative motif of the new order, and out over the flat
Yucatán plain new cities were built. One of the greatest cities of
this Mayan renascence was Uxmal.

Uxmal had been first mentioned in the literature in 1834,[*]
then again in 1838 when Waldeck published his beautiful but
inaccurate folio.[†] Since they had visited Uxmal before, it was
the first ruin to which the expedition of Stephens, Catherwood,
and Cabot made their way, after a few weeks spent in Mérida.
They established themselves in one of the vaulted rooms of the
House of the Governor, a large rectangular structure, pierced by
eleven doorways and decorated by a stone frieze, a mosaic com-

---

[*] Lorenzo de Zavala, *Antiquities mexicaines*, Paris, 1834.
[†] *Voyage pittoresque*, Paris, 1838.

posed of geometric motifs, a gigantic counterpoint that circled the entire structure. After the ruins had been cleared of most of the shrub jungle by the workmen, Catherwood made first a general map of the site and then a plan of the House of the Governor, which was so complete that Stephens said, 'Mr. Catherwood made minute architectural drawings of the whole, and has in his possession the materials for erecting a building exactly like it.' [2] Uxmal covered an area of two square miles. Its buildings, dominated in height at least, by a truncated pyramid with a barbarically beautiful building on its top—the House of the Magician—looked over a land so flat that every amorphous mound could be seen plainly. Not long after their arrival at Uxmal, Dr. Cabot and Stephens were stricken by malaria and were carried delirious to a near-by convent. Catherwood, left alone, worked for six weeks in Uxmal, completing more than fifty drawings. He found in Uxmal evidence that definitely linked these cities with those of Copán and Palenque, discovering a wooden lintel, made from *sapote* wood, on which was carved the same type of glyphs that they had seen at the other Mayan sites. This lintel—the only dated sculpture at Uxmal—which would have determined the date at which the city had been built, was brought back later to New York.

Uxmal, dating, by legend at least, from the ninth century, was famed as a religious center of the League of Mayapán. The ruins of this city-state, still in remarkable preservation, gave Catherwood, now a master at drawing Mayan art, full scope for his work. He surveyed Uxmal more completely than he had any of the other lands of his exploration. Here there was no lofty jungle. With the whole of the Maya civilization as the subject for his canvas, he set about the work of immortalizing the Mayas and 'F. Catherwood, Archt.' Catherwood's finest work was done at Uxmal; it was his happiest period. While he painted, Stephens and Dr. Cabot moved around the countryside, searching for new ruins 'worthy of Mr. Catherwood's talents.' When they returned after having found other ruins, the first thing they saw was 'Mr. Catherwood standing on the platform of the Casa del Gobernador, the sole tenant of the ruins of Uxmal.' Stephens relates, 'He had a feeling of security from the tranquil state of the country, the harmless character of the Indians and their superstitions in regard to the ruins, and a spring pistol with a cord across the door, which could not fail to bring down anyone who might attempt to enter at night . . . he had accomplished an enormous deal.'

But Catherwood suffered from all this daemonic activity. On New Year's day 1842, after six weeks of work, he was carried from the ruins of Uxmal, in complete delirium as a result of malaria.

2 : *KABAH, LABNÁ, SAYIL, BOLONCHEN, AND SABACHTSCHÉ*

In an archaeological tour that has been duplicated but once in a century, the group found ruin following ruin buried behind the dry Yucatán jungles. At Kabah, a site not far from Uxmal, they found other temples, built during the same period, but utterly different in design. On one temple six tiers of stone masks, open-mouthed with red tongues, contained the whole stone frieze, and dividing it was a bold medial molding, 'a scalloped and zig-zag band ingeniously put together of smaller pieces of stone with space enough to allow for the added play of light and shade on the pattern.' * So impressed was Catherwood by the design that he copied it faithfully and used it as binding decoration for *Incidents of Travel in Yucatán*, Stephens' book. At Kabah,

---

* 'And in homage to these pioneer explorers,' writes Pál Kelemen in his monumental *Medieval American Art,* 'it was also chosen to border the book jacket of this survey.'

Stephens discovered two remarkable sculptured doorjambs, six feet high, weighing over a half ton. These, being movable, were taken down by the Indians, tied to poles run down their center, and carried away. Catherwood made this episode the subject of one of his lithographs (Plate XVI); Stephens, in blue cutaway jacket, is seen directing their removal. These stones had a curious odyssey.[3]

After Kabah came the ruins of Sayil, which is one of the deepest spreading buildings in Yucatán, three stories high broken up into eighty rooms, its outside walls decorated with the long-snouted motif of the God Itzamna; and after Sayil, the site of Sabachtsché.

Near Sayil they stumbled onto the ruins of Labná, another of the League of Mayapán constellation and contemporaneous with Uxmal. There was a palace mounted on an earth podium, facing a large plaza, and ornamented with columnettes and masks several stories high. Catherwood made an elaborate drawing of the 400-foot-long building and another, an exact sketch of a most unusual structure, the Labná Gateway. He was much impressed with this portal arch at Labná. Of it he made one of his finest drawings.

In this manner, traveling lightly, the archaeological tour penetrated deep into Yucatán, across the unmarked border into Tabasco. Again ruin followed ruin. And to each, when possible, Catherwood gave his attention. South of Mayapán they came to the Bolonchen, 'Nine Wells of Yucatán.' A half-league from the village there was an abrupt opening in the limestone face; within this immense opening was the labyrinthine entrance into the wells of Bolonchen. All Yucatán derived its water from such underground *cenotes*. At Bolonchen, the natives descended a huge ladder, 120 feet under the surface, to get their water. It was a scene worthy of a Salvator Rosa, and Catherwood, eager to seize on a subject so picturesque, descended with easel and brushes and, there in the dripping darkness, sketched one of the most amazing sepias of his collection.

3 : CHICHÉN ITZÁ

In March 1842 (after a visit to the walled Mayan city of Tulum) they stood in the shadowed chamber that crowned the pyramid of Kulkulkan and looked down upon the fabled religious city of Chichén Itzá. The Mouth of the Wells, Itzá, derived its name from the two gigantic-mouthed *cenotes*, from which the city-state of Chichén Itzá once obtained its water. It was only a small colony during the Old Empire, but between the tenth and thirteenth centuries, when the peninsula was reoccupied and the whole of the Mayan civilization was contained on the flat lime-stone peninsula of Yucatán, Chichén Itzá became the most splendid city in the Maya area. They found an immense pyramid, then called El Castillo, a small but lavishly decorated building with the motifs of the long-nosed god. There was a *Caracol*, the use of which Stephens and Catherwood could not guess, but which is now known as an ancient observatory: one of the rare 'round' structures of the Maya area. They walked in the Temple of the Warriors, perplexed by all the columns, and visited the Ball Court, which they called (and quite correctly) the gymnasium. What they did not know, or was beyond their knowledge, they described in simple and intelligent terms. And all that Catherwood observed he figured in sepia, with his usual fidelity; dramatic, picturesque, yet utterly reliable. Few photographs give a better feeling of the intricate carving of Chichén Itzá than the huge lithographs that Catherwood, in 1844, worked out so carefully. These were the first drawings ever made of Chichén Itzá, and they are in a class, in number and quality, with Catherwood's work at Copán, Palenque, and Uxmal. These explorers correctly gauged what they

80

saw; they sensed that the people who built Copán in Honduras, Palenque in Mexico, also built Chichén Itzá. Thus Stephens and Catherwood prepared a *Baedeker* for future archaeologists.

On 17 June 1842, the expedition to the Maya came to an end.

Chapter Eight

THE VIEWS OF ANCIENT
MONUMENTS

What was this spiteful demiurge that always seemed to be in attendance on Frederick Catherwood? In the beginning, in July 1842, there was, it is true, little indication of the personal tragedy that would soon overtake Catherwood, for on his return to New York with Stephens and Cabot he had been acclaimed in the newspapers and commissioned at once to undertake, as he had in the previous publication, all the illustrations of Stephens' projected book, *Incidents of Travel in Yucatán.* In his absence the Panorama had prospered, and Mr. George Jackson was able to show a commendable profit from the constant flow of visitors into the Rotunda. Then, to stimulate an interest in their new discoveries, Catherwood had brought to the Rotunda the collections from Yucatán, the carved 'talking lintels' of Kabah and Uxmal, the stone sculptures, and beautiful vases. These, along with oversized watercolors of the Mayan ruins, were put on exhibition within the Panorama. The public had scarcely time to see them, when, on the night of 31 July 1842, after closing time, the Rotunda took fire.

Philip Hone, the diarist, was an eyewitness:

Catherwood's Panorama of Thebes and Jerusalem were burnt last evening about ten o'clock and those two valuable paintings were destroyed together with the other contents of the building, among which were a large collection of curiosities and relics and other pre-

82

cious things collected by Messrs. Stephens and Catherwood in their recent travels in Central America. This will be a severe loss not only to enterprising travellers, but to science and the arts in general. The edifice being perfectly circular and without windows and the contents of a peculiarly inflammable nature, the appearance of the conflagration was like that of a huge cauldron.[1]

Up, consumed by flames, went all of the Yucatán collections; utterly consumed were the priceless and irreplaceable Mayan wooden lintels with their carved hieroglyphics; up in smoke, too, went a huge section of Catherwood's life. The personal loss was calamitous.

New York papers, the next day, announced the Panorama's destruction:

DESTRUCTION OF THE ROTUNDA BY FIRE

A few moments after closing of this building in Prince Street last evening [31 July, 1842] at half past nine o'clock, it was discovered to be on fire, and in less than half an hour, owing to the combustible state of the paintings and other materials in it, the interior was entirely consumed *including* the panoramas of Jerusalem and Thebes. In addition to this loss by Messrs. Catherwood and Jackson, the owners, the former met with an almost invaluable loss in the total destruction of a large portion of his ancient relics and *original paintings*, obtained and produced while on his visits to Mexico and the surrounding country. The walls of the building remained standing although the heat was so severe that they cracked open in several places. The inside of the building with the circular wall enclosing the flames after the roof had fallen in, presented the appearance of a great fiery furnace. Mr. Catherwood had left the building but a short time previous to the fire, and had secured the building from damage as was supposed. A story was told among the crowd that the building was struck by lightning, but a gentleman who was standing on the corner of Prince Street when the flames were discovered, informed us that such was not the fact. The presumption is that it caught from some spark issuing from the lights inside that had been used in the course of the evening at the exhibition. The total loss is estimated at over $20,000 but a very small portion of which is insured. The building, as well as its contents, we understand, belonged to Messrs. Catherwood and Jackson, who are the sole sufferers. We trust the liberal city of our citizens will cause it to rise like Phoenix from its ashes.[2]

It continued the story the following day:

THE FIRE AT CATHERWOOD'S

This fire is likely to prove much more disastrous than we at first anticipated. For we find that Messrs. Catherwood and Stevens [Stephens] returned to this city from their last trip to Central America, they deposited all their valuable collections of curiosities, pieces of the ruins, specimens, drawings, plans * and everything that they had collected in their painful and perilous tour. These things are a great loss; no money can replace them. Mr. Catherwood thinks that if the water had been directed as he had desired at the fire these things might have been saved. He was insured for only $3,000. His own private loss will be at least $10,000 more.[3]

This was the end of established permanent panoramas in New York City. Catherwood's was the first and the last.

The fates had been unkind to Catherwood. His great work on the Dome of the Rock (Mosque of Omar) left unpublished, his pioneer work among the Egyptian tombs swallowed up in the anonymity of the unpublished folios of Robert Hay, and now his great work on the Maya in great part destroyed. Yet Catherwood did not allow his misfortune to possess him. Fortunately for him, many of his drawings had been given to the Harper & Brothers' engravers, and these, with his archaeological notebook and other sketches in his home at 89 Prince Street, had survived. So to assuage his wounds he threw himself into the making of Stephens' book. Harper & Brothers turned over to Catherwood the complete control of the illustrations and the design of the book on Yucatán, as it is stated in its special preface: '. . . the

* This destruction of many of Catherwood's drawings accounts doubtlessly for the paucity of his original material. Of the hundreds of beautiful sepias, water-colors and pencilings, less than twelve have been located.

illustrations were made from Daguerreotype views and drawings taken on the spot by Mr. Catherwood and the engravings executed under his personal superintendence.' Catherwood was forced to go through the whole roster of the National Academy of Design to find sufficient engravers. Prud'homme, Paris-trained, was the finest of contemporary engravers and did the best work. Alfred Jones, who had engraved many of William Mounts' pictures, was given the more delicate outline material; Johnson, Graham Halbert, Jordan, John A. Rolph, and J. M. Gimbrede,[4] all well-known engravers, worked under Catherwood's supervision. The illustrations, as might be expected from the dispatch of the work, were too hastily executed to be excellent, of too many hands to be uniform; *Incidents of Travel in Yucatán*, with its 120 engravings, was produced in six months; it was off the press and in the bookstores by March 1843.*

This new *Incidents of Travel*, sent to William H. Prescott by Stephens, served as Catherwood's introduction to Mr. Prescott, who was then putting the last words to his *Conquest of Mexico*. Prescott was deeply impressed with both the text and illustrations of *Yucatán*, and as soon as he had unfolded Catherwood's great panoramic drawing of Uxmal that illustrated the first volume, he said, 'it opens rich and promising.'

It was at this point that a new publishing venture was launched by Stephens and Catherwood. It was to be on so monumental a scale that only Audubon's vast folios of his *Birds of America* could stand as a bibliographical measure to it. The projected work was to be a huge, all embracing study of Central American archaeology. The idea began with a letter, dated 25 March 1843, from Stephens to Prescott:

---

* The binding of the *Incidents of Travel in Yucatán* reflects Catherwood's interest in Maya design. For the back of the binding he chose the Serpent motif from the Nunnery quadrangle at Uxmal; for its side the fretted motif from the ruins of Kabah; and in the center of the binding the circular serpent-decorated 'basket' from the 'Basket Ball' court at Chichén Itzá.

. . . A few words upon a new subject. I am thinking of sending out a prospectus for publishing by subscription, a great work on American Antiquities to contain 100 or 120 engravings fol. to be issued in four numbers quarterly. *Price $100!* Nine hundred subscribers will save me from loss, which is all I care for. I have no room for details and can only say that Mr. Catherwood has made several large drawings, which in the grandeur and interest of the subjects and in picturesque effect are far superior to any that have ever appeared. It is intended that the execution shall be creditable to the country as a work of art. From the specimens of engravings which we have seen of Audubon's new works [he had issued a smaller edition of his *Birds of America* in seven octavo volumes] we think that ours can be done in this country; if not, Mr. Catherwood will go over to Paris and have them executed there. Hon. Albert Gallatin [Jefferson's Secretary of the Treasury and in his later years an excellent ethnologist] will furnish an article, and he will endeavour to procure one from Humboldt with whom he formed an intimate acquaintance while Minister to France. I have written to Mr. [John] Murray . . . requesting him to apply to Sir John Wilkinson the best authority on all points of resemblance between American signs and symbols and those of Egypt. . . The fourth and only other person to whom I have thought of applying is yourself. I do so purely as a matter of business and in my estimate of expenses have allowed $250. and a copy of the work for an article from you. It need not contain more than 20 or 30 of your octavo pages and will not be wanted in less than a year.[5]

The project was grandiose, even at this distance. Even the mere prospect of bringing together in one work Humboldt, Prescott, Gallatin, Wilkinson, and Stephens with 120 drawings of Catherwood still stirs one's soul. For the period, the cost of the work to its patrons was staggering; to obtain an idea of its relative cost now, one must multiply it sixfold. Prescott, to suggest the high esteem in which he held both Stephens and Catherwood, replied by the next mail, 'The *American Antiquities* . . . is a noble enterprise, and I hope it may find patronage . . . I will supply an article of the length you propose.'[6]

The 'great project' began under excellent circumstances; Albert Gallatin called a meeting on 2 May 1843 of the executive committee of The New-York Historical Society, in order that they might consider giving the project their endorsement and sponsorship. Catherwood's drawings were exhibited in the library, and Stephens, in rare form, explained the project. Thereafter the venerable Albert Gallatin took over. Although eighty years of age and still speaking with the slightest trace of French accent, a heritage of his Swiss birth, Gallatin did not permit his debility to curb his enthusiasm. 'Stephens,' he said, 'having accomplished his principal task, of giving to the world a full, graphic and faithful description of these ruined cities and temples, now proposes to complete his valuable contributions to the cause of Historical and Scientific research by publishing an edition of the drawings on the scale here represented . . .' and he pointed out to the executive committee the fifteen large watercolors that Catherwood had made of the ruins, a fraction of the intended number that were to grace the work. 'This would certainly be a work,' Gallatin went on, 'in which every American must feel a just pride, and it ought, in fact, to be considered a national production.' He then asked that the New-York Historical Society sponsor the 'great project.' A series of resolutions were formulated in which was stressed the important fact 'that the recent discoveries of ruined cities and the remains of a people and history entirely unknown had given a new aspect to the American continent.' Professor Edward Robinson, a member of the committee and the founder of Palestinian archaeology,[7] who was intimately familiar with Catherwood's work in the East, enthusiastically seconded the resolutions, feeling that their publication would have an important bearing upon the character and reputation of the country. William B. Lawrence, vice president of the society, rose to make the final affirmative; he felt that the great project was calculated to call forth the highest enthusiasm and that the works of Stephens and

87

Catherwood would create a new era in the science of ethnology. Pointing to the large Catherwood drawings, he said: 'they afforded means of solving doubts and testing theories with regard to the origin of these races which inhabited the continent at the time of its discovery by Europeans.'

The drawings are not only to be admired as works of art but are replete with valuable information. . . How many have travelled hundreds of miles to visit the ruins of Paesteum, yet which of these fifty cities [of the Maya] now unveiled to the civilized world by Mr. Stephens, does not really present more interest than those isolated columns, even *Petra*, with the other wonders, disclosed in the glowing narrative which first brought [Mr. Stephens] to the notice of his countrymen, and gained for him so honorable a name, in the annals of literature; even the pyramids of Egypt, remarkable as was their magnitude as works of art, were inferior to these American antiquities, and lost their pre-eminent significance when contrasted with the colossal structures of Uxmal.

In closing, William Lawrence 'predicted that Stephens and Catherwood, the first investigators in this field, would be followed by hundreds of others and that though the fame gained for their distinguished countryman for his former volumes, was scarcely second to that of any name in our literary annals, he was destined, as a discoverer of these hidden treasures, to a still more exalted position.' [8] In a glowing tribute to Catherwood,[9] Albert Gallatin closed the session, thanking the members for their endorsement of a work that would take its place beside Audubon's immortal *Birds of America*.

Thus nobly launched, the 'great project' sailed out into the disturbed commercial waters of the United States. The time was not wholly propitious. The turbulent political scene that was climaxed with a fight between President Tyler and his own Whig party led by Daniel Webster had reflected uncertainty in the financial world, 'Manifest Destiny' the shibboleth under which the United States was to launch a war of aggression upon Mexico, gaining thereby ten millions of acres of real estate (and the enmity of the Latin-American world), had already been formulated. When James K. Polk took office in 1845, the fever of expansion would completely possess the body politic.

At first Harper & Brothers, Stephens' publishers, toyed with the idea of becoming the publisher of this, but, as they said in newspaper releases, they were 'not willing to undertake so great a work without some prospect of remuneration'; if 300 subscribers could be obtained at $100 each, Harpers would undertake it.[10] But 300 subscribers not being forthcoming, Harper & Brothers dropped the project. Then it was taken up at once by Bartlett & Welford and, in an attempt to awaken public interest, Catherwood's dramatic drawings were exhibited in bookstores and societies throughout the Eastern seaboard. On 3 June 1843, they were exhibited at the bookstore of Tappan & Dennet in Boston.[11]

Now Catherwood could well curse his star; the number of requisite subscribers could not be found, and even John Lloyd Stephens, obsessed by some soul-disturbing problems in his immediate family (and pressure from that ogre, politics), seemed to be losing interest. This time Catherwood resolved that he *would publish* and not allow, as in the case of his Mosque of Omar drawings, his Maya work to be usurped by others; in July, after consultation with William H. Prescott in Boston, Frederick Catherwood sailed to England.

American antiquities had drawn Prescott and Catherwood into intimacy, for Prescott, struggling through the morass of Central America, when writing *The Conquest of Mexico*, had been helped immeasurably by Stephens and confirmed in his deductions by Catherwood. Working half-blind among the manuscripts he had gathered from the dark corners of the world's libraries, he, too, had come to the conclusion that the American civilization was indigenous to the continent and that the structures that had been discovered in Central America were built by these civilizations. Prescott, as Stephens and Catherwood had done, completely rejected the idea of the American Indian having his origin out of misty voyages of Phoenicians, the Lost Tribes of Israel, or wandering Carthaginians. He was delighted that his views on the ruins had been reaffirmed by Catherwood. So he was willing to assist him in his new project. Prescott wrote a note of introduction to Edward Everett, the American Minister to the Court of St. James's, confiding in a letter dated 15 June 1843, that,

> . . . A literary project of some magnitude is set on foot here by Messrs. Stephens and Catherwood. It is the publication of the magnificent drawings made by Mr. Catherwood of the ruins of Central America. The intention is to have them engraved on a scale corresponding to that of the original designs. Mr. Catherwood will embark for Europe in July to confer with the English publishers who have intimated a willingness to be interested in the undertaking. I have taken the liberty to give him a note to you, at his desire. . . Mr. Catherwood, who is truly modest and a well-instructed man, desires only to have your approbation of this important undertaking and the interest you take in every liberal enterprise of your countrymen will, I have no doubt, interest you in the success of this. . .[12]

In London and again in the Catherwood house at 21 Charles Square, Hoxton, from which his brother, Alfred, carried on his medical practice, the artist of the Mayas, portfolio in hand, went out to bookseller and publisher. He met with little encouragement. This was a strange reception for so original a work, since it was the age of the illustrated book and of handsome folios of hand-colored lithographs. Not many years before, with much success, D. T. Egerton had published his *Views in Mexico,** and John Bateman, his magnificent book on tropical orchids.† Even at that

---

* *Views in Mexico; being a series of Twelve colored Plates of (Mexican Views)*, 1840. Published and drawn by D. T. Egerton. London, 1840.
† *The Orchidaceae of Mexico and Guatemala*, 40 magnificent color plates of orchids. London, Ackermann, 1843.

time, George Catlin was in London making final arrangements for the publication of his lithographic portfolio of American Indians.* Despite this, Catherwood was rebuffed. He wrote to Prescott:

> As regards the large work of Stephens and myself, nothing has been finally agreed on. The booksellers say trade is bad etc., the old story and I fear a very true one. . . I delivered your letter to Mr. Everett who received me very cordially but I have not yet attained my object, an audience of the Queen and Prince Albert. It would seem nowadays that nothing is successful here with the rich and aristocratic without the patronage and sanction of royalty which ill accords with my loco foco notions.

While Catherwood tried to find a sponsor for the great work on Central America, he undertook at the same time to assist Prescott in finding a British engraver to illustrate a new edition of *Ferdinand and Isabella*. A lively correspondence developed, and from the letters recently discovered in the Prescott collections of the Massachusetts Historical Society, Frederick Catherwood reveals his disappointment. Stephens had decided for reasons not clear (since the Stephens-Catherwood correspondence is lost) to withdraw entirely from the 'great project.' Catherwood explained to Prescott: 'My own work (for Stephens has declined having anything to do with it) is getting on, barely several of the plates are finished in the best style of lithography and others are in hand. I have no publisher and do not intend to have one this side at least . . . I shall be my own Publisher.' [13] He gathered together six of England's outstanding lithographers, Andrew Picken, Warren, Parrott, Bourne, Thomas Shotter Boys, and George Moore, to lithograph his drawings. Andrew Picken was given the largest number of plates—ten in all—to lithograph since he was a superb artist. A pupil of Louis Haghe, he had won in 1835 the Isis Medal

---

* *Catlin's North American Indian Portfolio*, 25 color plates. London, 1844.

for drawings. Then he was forced by an attack of phthisis to retire to Madeira, where he did many fine drawings before returning to London. He was already dying when he finished the Catherwood drawings. Warren, who executed the next largest number of plates (seven) was an artist's artist, a perfect technician, but with a copyist's soul. William Parrott derived from a family of painters—and was much traveled on the Continent, where he specialized in architecture; he lithographed four of the most beautiful of Catherwood's Maya drawings. John C. Bourne, who lived in Adelphi and came from a large family of engravers and painters, lithographed but a single plate (VIII). Thomas Shotter Boys, easily the most famed, was given the 'House of the Magician' at Uxmal * to lithograph. He executed this in his most facile manner, for Boys had studied watercolor under Richard Bonnington and had just published, himself, a splendid portfolio of views of London.† Then pressed by Andrew Picken's illness, Catherwood secured George Belton Moore, the austere drawing master of the Royal Military Academy, to do the 'Las Monjas' (Plate XXI) at Chichén Itzá; this Moore did in a geometric style with a hardness of line that rather spoiled the *tonalité* of the whole.

We know, strangely enough, precisely what this work cost. 'My book' Catherwood wrote to Prescott 'consists of 25 plates and a Title Page' (the 'great project' of 120 plates with text by Humboldt, Prescott, Gallatin, Wilkinson, and Stephens, had narrowed down to this) and 'the estimate was £ 10 per plate making the total estimate £ 260'; but the actual cost for the plates eventuated into £ 307.10.0. This sum of $1500 was a large outlay for Catherwood, who only the previous year had lost his life's fortune in the burning of his Panorama. The printing of the work to be called *Views of Ancient Monuments in Central America, Chiapas,*

---

* The original of this plate is in the collections of the United States National Museum.
† *Views of London as It Is*, A Series of views of London Streets, by Thomas Shotter Boys, London, 1843.

and Yucatán was executed by Owen Jones ('an intimate friend of mine,' Catherwood wrote) at his studio at 9 Argyll Place, London. Owen Jones, now famous for his *Grammar of Ornament*, was the son of the celebrated Welsh antiquarian and had been a pupil of Vuilliamy. He had published his first work on the 'Alhambra' the previous year, a work that forced him to sell his patrimony to complete. Forced into all forms of remunerative art work, he consented to print Catherwood's *Views*. The imprint bears his name.

The publication had proceeded far enough along by December 1843 for Catherwood to send Prescott 'a few proofs of the work through Stephens.' This was in return for Prescott's gift of a copy of his *Conquest of Mexico*, of which Catherwood 'could almost wish the subject had need of less absorbing interest, that I might have had a prolonged pleasure of its perusal.' In this letter came the first indication that John Lloyd Stephens, who had promised to write the text for the *Views*, would not be able to do so. 'Mr. Stephens has kindly offered to write an introduction and the descriptions, but I fear they will scarcely be in time, as I am endeavouring to get [it] out by the beginning of March.' [14]

On 25 April 1844 *The Views of Ancient Monuments of Central America, Chiapas, and Yucatán* with its twenty-five lithographs, map, introductions, and descriptions, 'dedicated to John L. Stephens esq.' was published in London. Catherwood, who had been explorer, archaeologist, artist, author, then publisher, was finally a bookseller of his own work.

So, at the age of forty-five, Catherwood published his first and only book; it was limited to three hundred sets. The ordinary edition sold for 5 guineas, and a small number of hand-colored sets, delicately done by an expert hand, were issued at 12 guineas. Bartlett & Welford of the Astor House Book Shop became the American publishers of the work and took a number of copies. 'I have been doing very well so far with my book in London,'

Catherwood wrote in an unusually enthusiastic letter to Prescott, 'but look with anxiety to the accounts from your side. If they are favourable I shall be highly successful. Of my £ 12.12.0. copies [the hand-colored copies] I have sold considerably more than I expected.'

And unexpected, too, was the text from Catherwood's pen, for writing was not his *métier*, and there exists but a single other contribution to archaeology written by him. Scarcely a literary stylist—his brush was his eloquence—Catherwood's text is none-theless noteworthy. In a century in which antiquarians, through the published works of Lord Kingsborough and Count Waldeck, believed that the buildings discovered in the Central American jungles were the work of either Egyptians, Greeks, Carthaginians, or Semitic tribes, the conclusion of Frederick Catherwood in regard to their origin is astute; his conclusions have stood the test of a century of the spade and trowel of archaeology. Although he was possessed of neither the documents we have today nor the evidence of extensive excavations, the general outlines of Catherwood's conclusions remain unchallenged. In sum, they represent the modern position, with slight modifications, of Ameri-can archaeology today. He wrote in his introduction,

with regard to the various theories that have been formed to trace the nations that peopled the American continent, through their mi-grations to their original habitations in the Old World, we find them all resting for support upon a few vague similarities of rites and customs, more or less common amongst every branch of the human family. Besides the idea that civilization and its attendant arts, is in every case derivative and always owing to a transmission from a cultivated to an unpolished people, is eminently unphilosophical, as it only removes further back without explaining the original difficulty of Invention, which must somewhere have taken place. . . Mr. Stephens and myself, after a full and precise comparative survey of the ancient remains [concluded] . . . that they [the ruins] are not of immemorial antiquity, the work of unknown races; but that, as we now see them, they were occupied and possibly erected by the Indian tribes in possession of the country at the time of the Spanish conquest—that they are the production of an indigenous school of art, adapted to the natural circumstances of the country, and to the civil and religious policy then prevailing—and that they present but very slight and accidental analogies with the works of any people or country in the Old World.

In the whole range of literature on the Maya there has never appeared a more magnificent work than *Views of Ancient Monuments.*

After the publication of the *Views*, at the London meeting of the Royal Institute of British Architects (with his old friend, Thomas Donaldson, as chairman), Catherwood, with his drawings as a background, read to a distinguished group a paper, Antiquities of Central America.[15] Before this learned assembly Catherwood stressed that, before his explorations, it would have been considered a flight of fancy to suggest that the Mayas as builders 'were in no wise inferior to the Egyptians,' and that their painting could be regarded as superior to that of the Egyptians, and 'more nearly like the paintings found at Pompeii and Herculaneum.' This was a strong statement. Yet those present knew that Catherwood had spent ten years in the East and was qualified, as none other, to speak of comparative archaeology. Catherwood perorated on the manner in which the Mayas cut the stones, their knowledge of mortars, stuccoes, and cements; he entered into the architectural techniques and then explained the Mayan 'arch.' He called it this, as he said, because it answered the purpose of one. He felt that the Mayas were on the 'very threshold of discovering the true principles of the arch.' With regard to the age of these monuments, the secretary reported, 'Mr. Catherwood differed from Del Rio, Du Paix, Lord Kingsborough and Waldeck,' who would give them great age—almost an antediluvian antiquity. The amount of debris covering the ruins suggested 'nothing.' Catherwood did

95

not think he would be safe in ascribing to any of those monuments (which still retain their form) a greater age than 800 to 1000 years, and those perfect enough to be drawn more than 400 to 600 years. The accuracy of such deductions does much to gauge Catherwood's knowledge, for Copán is slightly over 1300 years old, Palenque, 1000, Uxmal, not much beyond 800, and the last archaeological additions to Chichén Itzá doubtlessly within the 600-year figure placed on it by Catherwood. It was just this calm judgment that led James Fergusson, the great architectural historian to rely on Catherwood's work when he attempted, in his *History of Architecture in all Countries*, to make something of the chaos of ancient American culture.

Hitherto the great difficulty had been that the drawings of American monuments—especially those published by Humboldt and the Lord Kingsborough—cannot be depended upon. The one bright exception to this censure are those of F. Catherwood, both those which he published separately, and those which he illustrated for the works of Mr. Stephens. Had that artist undertaken to classify his work in a chronological series, he doubtless could have done it; but as the arrangement of the plates is purely typographical and they are so far reduced to a common denominator by the process of engraving, the classifications can hardly now be attempted by one not familiar with the buildings themselves.[16]

In the meanwhile there seems no good reason for doubting the conclusion at which he and Mr. Stephens arrived: that the cities they rediscovered were those that were inhabited and in the full tide of their prosperity at the time of the Spanish conquest.

Such was Frederick Catherwood's position in the world of art, archaeology, and architecture. He had at long last come into his own. His *Views* was a success apparently and there was talk of doing a future work on Central America, which he discussed with Bartlett and Welford; and even Peru was mentioned. Peru was suggested as a new era for Catherwood's talents; 'Stephens tells me,' wrote Prescott, 'that you have talked of a trip to Peru. This is my ground [he was then beginning to write *The Conquest of Peru*] but I suppose it will not be the worse for your mousing into the architectural antiquities, and I wish I could see the fruits of such a voyage in your beautiful illustrations.' [17] It is always to be regretted that Catherwood did not act on this impulse. Certainly American archaeology would have been enriched. So well known in London was the figure of Frederick Catherwood lecturing before his drawings of the Central American ruins that Wilkie Collins had him in mind when in his novel *The Woman in White*, published in 1860, he had Walter Hartwright go to Central America in the 1850's to make architectural pictures for an archaeological expedition. And so famous was Catherwood's *Views* that when Alexander von Humboldt sent to Prince Albert, Consort of Queen Victoria, a copy of his *Kosmos*, Catherwood's work was chosen as a reciprocal gift to Humboldt. Prince Albert wrote to Humboldt on 17 February 1847,

I have been constantly impressed while gradually reading the first volume of your *Kosmos* with my desire to thank you for the high intellectual enjoyment its study has afforded me . . . to give some substantial character to the expression of my thanks, I present you the accompanying work, Catherwood's *Views in Central America*. It may serve as an appendix to your own great work on Spanish America and thus become worthy of your attention. . .* [18]

---

* Humboldt answered: . . . 'EW Königlichen Hoheit kann ich den innigsten Regungen meines Gemüthes Nachgebend, und jetzt im Besitz des herrlichen Geschenkes (der malerischen Darstellung räthselhafter Denkwerke amerikanischer Völker) nicht länger zögern meinen tiefgefühlten ehrerbietigsten Dank so Füssen zu legen. . . Humboldt, dated Potsdam, 19 April 1847. From an unpublished letter in the Royal Archives at Windsor Castle, reproduced with the special permission of His Majesty the King.

enough, was never exhibited: his famous sketch of 'View of New York City from Governors Island,'[2] an excellent watercolor of the New York sky line seen from the battlements of Governors Island, done with all the maturity of a skilled architectural draftsman. Engraved by Henry Papprill * in aquatint and hand colored, the 'View of New York City' is one of the finest and most pleasing of the period and is fervently sought as a collector's item. Although the original drawing has disappeared, the aquatint plate is still extant.

As expected, from the misfortunes that continued to follow him, Catherwood's efforts to secure large commissions ended in total defeat. He entered the contest for a fountain for Gramercy Park, and, calling upon his classical experience, designed one in the Renaissance manner, following 'a plan of one of the fountains erected in front of St. Peter's Church in Rome, which are acknowledged to be the most beautiful in Europe.' The cost, estimated at $5300, staggered the city fathers when Catherwood, portfolio in arm, appeared before them. He was refused the commission. Two years later a fountain of more modest design was erected.[3]

His design for a statue of Washington followed the familiar Catherwood fortune. When a contest was announced he quickly entered it. Art patrons in New York City had agitated for a suitable heroic monument to Washington for many years, and the newly formed Washington Monument Association with Colonel John Trumbull as president was established in 1843. Funds were provided by a subscription list, and in June 1844 Calvin Pollard, a New York architect, began a design of a gothic tower 425 feet high—'for myself,' as he modestly said: yet had it engraved and issued it as a broadside. Robert Kerr submitted a design of a

---

* Henry Papprill, an excellent engraver of this period, has no known personal art history. He worked in the period 1844-60, but he is known actually for only two aquatints, one the Catherwood 'View' and the other 'New York from St. Paul's Steeple,' drawn by J. W. Hill.

Washington monument in classic style, a round marble temple with Corinthian columns; Catherwood working with Thomas G. Crawford and Henry Hillyard, conceived a heroic statue of Washington, 75 feet high mounted on a huge stone pedestal that was itself to be 55 feet in height. Not to be outdone by Pollard, the design was lithographed by Thomas and circulated among members of the Committee. The City Fathers, still impressed by the pinnacled fantasies of the 'Gothic,' rejected Catherwood's design and awarded the contract to Minard Lafever. Yet when the monument to George Washington was finally erected in Union Square in 1856, it was Catherwood's pedestal design they used.[4]

But of American archaeology for which Catherwood and John Lloyd Stephens were directly responsible, both had little more concern. Stephens had become a member of New York Constitutional Convention; he had taken part in the foundation of the Hudson River Rail-Line, and now he was going to Europe on the *S.S. Washington* to inaugurate the first direct ocean traffic between New York and the port of Bremenhaven.

However, these Maya discoverers did put aside their business activities long enough to become founder members of the American Ethnological Society.[5] In April 1845, just before he left for South America, Catherwood found time to prepare a scholarly paper on the antiquities of Tunis, 'Punico-Libyan Monument at Dugga,' which he read before the Society.[6] A few months later it was published in the first volume of the publication of the American Ethnological Society. It was his second and last publication.

Then Catherwood disappeared into South America.

Chapter Ten

RAILROADS AND GOLD POKES

I : *BRITISH GUIANA*

By the winter of 1845, once again in London, the protean Mr. Catherwood made his final transfigurement; he became an engineer, more specifically a railroad builder. His various professions —draftsman, architect, classicist, architectural-explorer, panoramist, archaeologist—had kept pace with the shifting moods of the times. Catherwood's training, basically sound and broad in concept, allowed him this shift in emphasis. The title of architect— he always wrote it Arch^t which he had proudly placed at the end of his name on every conceivable occasion, now disappeared; henceforth he was '*F. Catherwood, C.E.*'

As Civil Engineer, Catherwood worked on the building of the Sheffield-Manchester Railway and, seemingly, on other railway projects in the United States. In the autumn of 1845 he was summoned to London before the Committee of Management of the Demerara Railway Company and offered a contract for surveying the first railroad in South America. 'The committee,' said the official report, 'consider that they have been particularly fortunate. Mr. Catherwood, the gentleman they have engaged, resided for some years in North America, where he was employed upon railroads and extensive public works; and at the time of his services offered to the Company, he was professionally engaged upon a railway in this country.' [1] Engaged for one year to make a survey of the proposed railway, Catherwood sailed for British Guiana

17 November 1845. And this now makes intelligent his own cryptic statement: 'I was obliged to absent myself for several years on a professional engagement in the West Indies.' [2] Arriving in British Guiana in December of the same year, with the professional aplomb acquired with his new position in life, he surveyed the problems of the first railway to be built on the South American continent.

British Guiana (bordering Venezuela) had been taken from the Dutch in 1803. England had had some sentimental claim to the Guianas ever since Sir Walter Raleigh explored them in hope of finding there, or on its jungle fringe, the treasures of El Dorado. English planters from the West Indian islands soon settled, with their slaves, the East Coast, principally along both banks of the Demerara River. In 1845 it was proposed that a railway be built to operate between Georgetown and Mahaica in order that the planters could market easier the sugar cane and cotton from their plantations. A prospectus was issued for a Demerara East Coast Railway to be capitalized for £ 100,000, and a representative dispatched to London. There in the City they had little difficulty in establishing the project whose capitalization was raised to £ 250,000; whereafter 10,000 shares at £ 25 were quickly disposed of. On the Board of Directors were sons of Gladstone and Sir Robert Schomburgk, the famous explorer of British Guiana; it was this organization that chose Catherwood.

For six months Catherwood explored the projected line of the railroad, following the entire length of the East coast of Demerara between Georgetown, the capital of the colony, and the village of Mahaica, the terminus of the railroad. Along this route, between the tangling jungle and the tropical sea coast, Catherwood proposed to lay down the lines of his railroad. His twenty-page report was an excellent survey, so professional in tone that it is hard to believe that this was the man who for at least twenty years of his life was wholly an archaeological explorer.

After his survey in British Guiana he left for Jamaica, where he inspected the recently constructed Kingstown and Spanish Town Railway. He wanted to make a thorough investigation so that he might, as he wrote, 'escape their errors.' He then left for the United States and 'examined' as he writes, 'many of the principal lines in operation there.' He ended the survey by determining the price of materials he proposed to buy in North America. He then returned to London and completed a detailed cost report, signing it with his new title: 'F. Catherwood, C.E.' The London Committee of Management was most impressed with the report when they met again on 15 April 1847 in Old Jewry Chambers in London. Not only because of this report with its detailed estimates, but for other reasons, Catherwood went far beyond his mission; he drew up a plan for drainage of the rail-line on the cotton estates, and submitted a detailed suggestion for the establishment of a central factory for distilling sugar cane to obviate the number of smaller ones, which each of the fifty-five plantations possessed individually and operated at great expense.[3] After reading 'Mr. Catherwood's very able report,' Mr. Charles Cabe, the chairman of the group, who dreamed his *sueños dorados*, and of the wealth to be theirs in the building of the railway, informed his committee that 'it will be satisfactory to the Shareholders to learn that . . . they have resumed the engagement with Mr. Catherwood by which his exclusive services have been secured to the company.' Confirmed in his appointment with full powers as superintendent, Catherwood returned on one of the Royal-Mail steam packets to British Guiana. There on 16 March 1846, His Excellency, Henry Light, the Resident-Governor of the Crown Colony, congratulated '. . . a scientific gentleman who proposed remaining in the colony for some time. . . . Mr. Catherwood who had attained some eminence as a scientific traveller and who had come out to superintend the progress of the Demerara Railway Co.'[4]

So the railway began—or paradoxically—so it did not begin.

Labor troubles they had at once. It was difficult to obtain labor even at a dollar a day. Negroes who worked on the plantations at a fraction of this sum had little incentive to leave them to work at the higher pay. The London committee thought—with a capitalist's naïvete—'that the novelty of the work would attract many living in the vicinity of Georgetown.' Within six months this novelty, if it existed, was no more. Then there were the termites. These isopterous insects with a voracious appetite for wood found the pitchpine sleepers, which Catherwood had brought from Savannah, precisely attuned to their cellulose appetites. They began upon them as soon as they were laid.

The rail line had hardly gone two miles in a year and under the strain Frederick Catherwood began to exhibit a marked change in character. Constant exposure to a tropical climate with a continuous repetition of malarial fever began to aggravate his querulousness. This had been evident previously in Central America when he traveled with Stephens, but it was never openly indicated in Stephens' pages. Now, frustrated by climate and man, Catherwood showed himself singularly unpleasant when he was crossed; 'There was,' said an official report,[5] 'considerable disagreement' with Catherwood over the rail line running on the river frontage, but the local gentry gave way to Mr. Catherwood; there was 'considerable disagreement' on the location of the site of the terminus in Georgetown; and when the Local Committee opposed Catherwood's selection there was 'considerable perturbation' when they discovered that 'Catherwood had been given full powers to act independently of the Local Committee.' Although the planters liked the thoroughness of Catherwood's performance in the face of rising difficulties,* his affronts to the colony increased with alarming frequency. For one thing the official ceremonies: 'His

---

* 'Mr. Catherwood appears to have been very thorough in his methods, as while carrying out his survey he was at the same time supervising various experiments, among others with regard to pile driving, shrinkage of embankments, enlargements of trenches, use of *pegass* [peat discovered by Catherwood in the

Excellency, Governor Light, felt that there should be an imposing ceremony worthy of the occasion of turning the sod for the *first railway ever* on the great South American continent and a silver plated shovel and wheelbarrow was ordered in London.' As these symbols of progress did not arrive at the right moment, it was decided that His Excellency would turn the first sod in a private manner only in the presence of Executive Committee but

this arrangement was, however, spoiled by the Chief Engineer, Mr. Catherwood, who issued a few invitations much to the annoyance of the Chairman, who then himself gave orders for the issuance of an additional number. In the end the ceremony was neither strictly private nor was it public . . . and the local shareholders who had been invited to attend, expressed their dissatisfaction in no uncertain terms.

Thus Catherwood's poltergeist was already undermining another of his projects.

The arrival of the first locomotives to operate on the completed three-and-a-half miles of rail line were promptly named by Catherwood, 'The Mosquito,' 'The Sandfly,' and 'The Fire Fly.' * Operating at once on the tracks it was by many years the first active line in South America. It would be some years before William Wheelwright, American, would build his railroad in Chile and long before Henry Meiggs, the prodigal *yanqui*, would fling a hundred tons of earth-torn metal across the Andes. But this priority in achievement did not solve the matters of either labor or money. Catherwood had inserted advertisements in the papers of Barbados and Jamaica, offering liberal wages and free passage to British Guiana. Soon after the arrival of the Negroes from Jamaica, however, the local gentry began to complain fiercely of

---

extensive savannah] as a fuel and the manufacture of bricks and pipes.' Sydney H. Bayley, in *Railways in British Guiana*, n.d.

* 'Years later,' says Sydney Bayley, 'these same three locomotives were renamed The Scorpion, The Centipede and The Marabunta. One wonders whether conditions in British Guiana at the time prompted the selection.'

the free use of the ladies of the colony by the migratory workers. So Frederick Catherwood had to arrange brothels in strategic areas along the route of the railroad. Bogged down with floods, flies, and floosies, a faint nostalgia for times past swept over Catherwood and in this mood he wrote to his old friend, John Russell Bartlett of the Astor House Book Store:

> Georgetown, Demerara
> Sept. 27, 1847

My Dear Bartlett,

As one of the Railway Company's vessels is about to leave for New York in a few days I take the opportunity of writing you a few lines.

I have been anxiously hoping to hear from you in answer to a letter I addressed you two or three months ago. I am not sure that it reached its destination but trust that it did. Should you be at a loss for sending your answer, Messrs. Howland and Aspinwall would take charge of any letter addressed to me, as they are in correspondence with our Committee here.

I shall be *very glad* of any news (not political *or relating to the Mexican War*) that you will be pleased to send me. I have heard nothing from Stephens and of him only that he went to England and returned forthwith. Neither has Mr. Griffin written, so that I am quite at a loss for the kind of news that most interest[s] me. I trust [you] therefore to send me a few lines forthwith. In regard to my operations here I am preparing the Terminus Building and commencing the embankment. Of course a new country like this is totally unaccustomed to work of this nature, everything goes slowly and only by the time the work is completed shall I have got together a good gang of workers. I had hoped to have had some of the carriage, trucks, etc. from the U.S. but freight being higher with you than in England and other circumstances has prevented it.

Tell me how business is going or whether you are publishing any more Books and if the Ethno. Society is in existence. How is Mr. Gallatin and many others? Have you been to England? How is Mrs. Bartlett and the Children? Have you been able to sell any more of copies of the Central America [*Views of Central America, Chiapas, and Yucatán*]? Here is an abundance of questions to answer and all of them interesting to me.

I suppose there is a good deal of building going on in N.Y. and perhaps I should have done better by stopping there than going to the W. I. [West Indies i.e. British Guiana] where everything is in a very depressed state and expense of living very high. You must not be surprised to see me back some day in New York and trying to start anew in business. . .

By 1849 Catherwood was desperately wishing for a change of scenery. The labor difficulties were insurmountable, and there was hardly any money left in the railroad's treasury. Pressing liabilities amounted to £ 36,300 and there were no immediate funds to meet the pay rolls. The line had got only as far as Plaisance, a distance of five-and-one-half miles at a cost of £ 127,000.* This made it the most expensive railroad ever built. Nor were matters helped by the death of Mr. Alex Wishart, one of the most popular men of the colony and one of the local committee, who was killed when the engine 'Sand-fly' passed over him. For although he obtained in death the dubious honor of being the first man killed in South America by a railroad engine, the accident did not raise the esteem of the colony for Mr. Catherwood, on whom they poured the blame for anything connected with the rail line.

In May 1849, Frederick Catherwood 'had drunk his drench.' He had had enough of railroads, enough of floosies, disagreements, termites, flies, and committees. Whether he resigned or was discharged we do not know, since he was relieved with the usual euphemism: 'Mr. Catherwood's agreement was terminated for reasons of economy.'

---

* The rail line was opened to Plaisance on 3 November 1848 to general traffic. There was no ceremonial opening, for the Directors remembered the 'first turning of the sod' and did not wish to repeat the performance.

2 : *PANAMÁ*

It was not in the ordering of the Fates that Catherwood should escape the railroads. He had hardly settled in Jamaica for a much needed rest when a letter came from John Lloyd Stephens begging him, in the name of their old friendship, to come to him in Panamá. He was urgently needed. For John Stephens had also acquired, in the interval, a railroad—a heroic project, the construction of forty-seven miles of track across the fetid Isthmus of Panamá. Stephens and two other New Yorkers, capitalists Henry Chauncey and William H. Aspinwall, had bought up the French franchise for 600,000 gold francs and contracted with the Republic of New Granada (Colombia) to construct a railroad across the isthmus. Financed for ten million dollars, guided by the enthusiasm of Stephens and the organization of shipping lines of Howland and Aspinwall, and backed by powerful persons in the United States Senate, led by Thomas Hart Benton, they moved down to the Atlantic side of the isthmus, at Limon Bay, and there on 2 May 1850 began to lay the first rail. Stephens, vice-president of the line, was the diplomat of the road, and, since he had to leave for Bogotá to negotiate with Colombia for changes in their contract, he had urgent need for Catherwood in the isthmus.

Only his deep-seated affection for Stephens could have forced Catherwood again into that tropical nightmare, but he heeded Stephens' plea. En route to Panamá he was seen by John Bigelow.*

On the banks of the tropical río Chagres, near the village of Gorgona, Stephens and Catherwood embraced. Both were deeply touched by the meeting. Now with his old friend in command,

---

* 'Among our fellow passengers [on the voyage down] was Mr. Catherwood, the artist, who was on his way to Central America whence after a sojourn of a few months he proposed to embark for California on a professional visit. His large experience as a traveller in every quarter of the globe rendered him an interesting and useful addition to our mess.' *Jamaica in* 1850, by John Bigelow (1817-1911), p. 4.

Stephens could leave, as Catherwood himself relates: 'Having completed my engagement in the West Indies, I rejoined Mr. Stephens to assist his great enterprise of spanning the isthmus with a road of iron and took charge of the works while he made a second journey to Santa Fe de Bogotá.' [6]

But in Panamá Catherwood was concerned with more than railroads. The isthmus swarmed with gold-seekers, California-bound, dressed in the accepted style of slouch hat, red shirt, cowhide boots, and Colt revolver. There was more to do than guide the building of the road and pay the workers; 'charge of the works' meant digging Americans out of difficulties, attending to fainting ladies, ladling out Homeric simples to those infected with the insidious malaria, and, when that failed, arranging burying parties to inter the mounting number of dead. There was in 1850 a historical meeting in Panamá amid all that fury of movement; Catherwood met a young man named Heinrich Schliemann,[7] who was bound for Sacramento, California, to take over the estate of his brother who had died a short time before of typhus. A curious meeting, for this same Schliemann, then only twenty-nine, would also, sometime later, become a famous archaeologist and discover the Homeric city of Troy. Schliemann was infected by the gold-fever and left for California on the S.S. Oregon. Catherwood, however, was suffering from something other than the gold virus; he had malaria. When Stephens returned from Bogotá, himself ill from a disease that shortly would become fatal, he found Catherwood deathly ill, so ill that he was unable to walk. He had to be carried to a ship bound for California. It was the last time they would meet.

3 : CALIFORNIA

Frederick Catherwood arrived at Yerba Buena—it had not yet become San Francisco—after a tidal wave of immigrants, bitten by the gold bug had raised its population to 50,000. It was the frenetic California of 1849. Fire had destroyed the waterfront, the false-fronted houses, saloons, and bawdy houses; the place was a charred mass. Yet the population of Yerba Buena—Chinese, Indians, Spaniards, Americans, Frenchmen, gold grubbers, merchants, gamblers, harlots and cutpurses, with a generous sprinkling of honest men—was scrambling about to raise a new city. It was the city of 'Honest' Harry Meiggs with his huge operations; Lt. William T. Sherman, taking a fling at banking; Lola Montez, and that able operator, Thomas O. Larkin, the first American Consul. Into this maelstrom of gold and confusion, Frederick Catherwood debarked; he took up his residence with Alfred Robinson, the west-coast representative of the Aspinwall's Pacific Mail Steamship Co. It was there, not many days later, that Catherwood, whether he willed it or not, became an American citizen. California became a State of the Union, and all inhabitants of California at that moment, by virtue of the admission of the new state, automatically became citizens of the United States of America. Despite his years, for he was now past the half-century mark, Catherwood's body, in the benign climate of California, mended quickly. He helped rebuild Yerba Buena, erected warehouses, and built wharves; later he sailed to Oregon Territory on one of William Aspinwall's side-wheelers, where he toured the interior, spending some weeks at the junction of the Columbia and Willamette Rivers. From Oregon he reported to the United States Government, 'Relative to the practicability of forming settlements on the Columbia River.' [8] This historic report has disappeared. Back in San Francisco in 1851, Catherwood was again mixed up in railroads and speculations; this time it was on a gigantic scale and it offered, so he thought, at least a chance to recoup all his losses. It involved the first projected rail line in the State of California, the Benecia-Marysville Railroad.

Benecia, 'The Queen City of the Bay,' then a settlement of

straggling huts in the straits of Carquinez, was marked by Thomas O. Larkin (who bought heavily in land around it) and his associates, Robert Hemple and General Mariano Vallejo, to be the principal port of the bay. It was a grandiose land scheme. Sacramento was to be displaced as the capital of the state by Marysville on the Feather River, and the promoters would wean the shipping from Yerba Buena, build a railroad from Benecia to Marysville, thereby cornering the devil's share of California's land and commerce. The first part of the operation was a building boom in Benecia. After much burning of midnight whale oil, Alfred Robinson, agent of the Pacific Mail, agreed to have its vessels moor at Benecia instead of Yerba Buena and to make it, the principal bay port; and well he might, for he too was involved in land speculation. William Aspinwall in New York was won over to the scheme, rather easily, since Yerba Buena's shallow anchorage was not liked by his sea captains anyway. Aspinwall then purchased a large tract of land on the shoreline of Benecia, including Mare Island, destined to become the Navy's great Pacific base. However, he placed a single important condition to the whole proposal: Benecia must be declared the official port of entry. As soon as the principal merchants in San Francisco (Yerba Buena) learned of the scheme, the 'war of the ports' developed. By that time Frederick Catherwood was part of it.

The promoters, well aware that Catherwood had had much to do with the developments of railroads elsewhere, made him an offer, which he accepted, and he was selected by Thomas Larkin to be consulting engineer to the project. William H. Aspinwall, who, of course, knew him very well, on 13 November 1850, wrote to Alfred Robinson: 'The appointment of Mr. Catherwood at Benecia is approved.' [9]

By 1852, the Benecia-Marysville Railway assumed corporate form; $8000 was set aside for the surveys and Frederick Cather-

wood became one of the Railroad's engineers.* At an estimated
cost of three million dollars and believed by its optimistic sponsors
capable of completion within two years, the stock, according to
the *Alta California*, had been 'readily taken up.' [10] In November
1852, the surveying party was at Marysville, stopping at the Merchants Hotel. By March 1853, the survey for the projected 85
miles of railway, which was to traverse the Green and Suisun
Valleys, crossing the Sacramento River on its way to Marysville,
was complete. In April 1853, a 'Report of the Engineer of the
Survey of the Marysville and Benecia Railroad' was issued. On
the last page, and until now unidentified by historians, was the
name:

> F. Catherwood,
> Consulting Engineer.

With high hopes, Catherwood purchased land in Benecia
heavily and threw what remained of his savings into the stock of
the rail line. He who had built the first rail line in South America,
superintended for a time the first transcontinental rail line on the
Isthmus, now, in the golden sun of California saw in the projected
first Californian railroad the transfiguration of F. Catherwood,
C.E. His health regained, his enthusiasm rekindled, he left San
Francisco in 1852, journeyed down to Acapulco, debarked, rode
across Mexico, re-embarked at Vera Cruz, and sailed to England.

---

* The surveying party was composed of William J. Lewis, Chief Engineer;
F. Catherwood, Consulting Engineer, L. B. Healy of Santa Clara, J. J. Lewis,
San José; Frederick Emory, Marysville, Assistant Engineers.

Chapter Eleven

'MR. CATHERWOOD ALSO
IS MISSING'

On its seventh day at sea, the *S.S. Arctic's* ugly hull was wholly obscured by a thick fog-blanket. And this was the first event of a featureless voyage. The *S.S. Arctic* left Liverpool bound for New York on 20 September 1854, carrying with her 385 passengers and crew; included in the list was 'F. Catherwood.' After two years in London,[1] he had settled his affairs, disposed of some of his pictures, and edited a new edition of Stephens' *Incidents of Travel in Central America*, to which he contributed a brief memoir of his friend, who had died in New York 12 October 1852. Then at Liverpool he caught the *Arctic* 'to return to his property in California.'

The *S.S. Arctic* was to make a landfall of Cape Race, Newfoundland, that day, and many passengers, mostly New Yorkers, were audible in their complaints about the opaque drop-curtain that veiled their first view of land. It was a gay group: the Duc de Grammont was returning to his diplomatic post in Washington; Mrs. Collins and her children, the family of Mr. E. K. Collins, the owner of the Collins Line, held court at the Captain's table; and one could, if one had a mind, pick out, on the 226 foot deck, the Drews, the Comstocks, the Fabbricottis, the Howlands, the Lockmiranets, the Ravenscrofts, and all the other notable names that ornamented the passenger list. The only serious note was a discussion of the war then waging between Russia and England;

Sebastopol had been under siege when they embarked from Liverpool, and it was a question discussed by the dilettante strategists with the top deck as the Crimea battlefield. But the thickening fog had put an end to this harmless military diversion and the men had retired to the main saloon. 'The pilot stood at the wheel,' said the Rev. Henry Ward Beecher, many days later reconstructing for his congregation the events that led up to the tragedy, 'the pilot stood at the wheel, but *death* stood upon the prow and no eye beheld him. Whoever stood at the wheel in all the voyage, Death was the pilot that steered the craft and none knew it.'

At noon the captain had just left the wheelhouse when he heard the watch call, 'Hard starboard.' Suddenly, without warning, another vessel, the *Vesta*, a French screw-propelled vessel, loomed out of the ocean. The watch had barely time to shout. The two vessels rammed head-on. Th*e Vesta* pulled away and listed badly. The Captain of the *Arctic* unaware of his own plight, stood by to help the passengers of the wrecked *Vesta*. Later the engineer appeared on deck in great agitation to report that the hull of the *Arctic* was badly punctured and its fires had already been extinguished. Everyone fell to manning the pumps. Slowly the *Arctic* settled in the stern. There were not enough lifeboats. The crew, rushing up from below, jumped at once into the available boats, lowered them, and pulled away from the ship. Within an hour the passengers were left to their own devices. Those who kept their wits tried to construct a huge raft out of timber and barrels. The First Officer, remembering a sinking ship's etiquette, raised the American flag upside down; Stewart Holland, a young engineer, began to fire the distress-cannon. When, after an hour's firing, they realized that they were a hundred or more miles from shore, he solemnly announced that he would fire it for the last time. 'The Last Gun' with Stewart Holland pulling the lanyard is the subject of a famous Currier & Ives print.

At five P.M., the *Arctic* sank with almost all of its complement of passengers. And then night mercifully dropped its veil.

Two weeks later the New York papers spilled out the news in their largest type:

THE LOSS OF THE ARCTIC

———— o ————

CAPTAIN LUCE SAFE

———— o ————

THRILLING ACCOUNT BY THE CAPTAIN

———— o ————

STATEMENT BY MR. GILBERT

———— o ————

SERMONS ON THE DISASTER.

As the death lists were posted, most of the New Yorkers stopped their work to begin a search of the newspapers. The Stock Exchange closed, banks stopped their business, flags throughout all the city were at half-mast. The Captain of the *Arctic* made his first statement from Quebec, where he was brought after he had been saved. It was addressed to Mr. E. K. Collins, president of the line: 'Dear Sir: It becomes my painful duty to inform you of the total loss of the *Arctic*, under my command, with your wife, daughter and son. . .' Then followed, day upon day, name after name of the missing passengers. For two weeks the dailies swept everything from the first page to bring the details of the tragedy that had taken three hundred lives.[2] The last movements of seemingly all aboard were described: Mrs. Child and daughter, of Springfield, Massachusetts, had come to the Captain to bid him an affectionate farewell. 'I saw Capt. Pratt and his Lady; they went down with all the rest.' Mr. Stone and family were on deck and went down with the rest. The Duc de Grammont made a spring into the First Officer's boat—Mr. Brown, Mr. Cahill, Mr. Allen, Mrs. Jones—'Mr. Baalham asked me if he should put his little boy in the boat. . .' One by one, the survivors told of the last acts of those who had perished, and later the newspapers printed long obituaries of each of the victims. All, that is, except Frederick Catherwood. Not a word of the friend of Keats, Severn, Shelley; and, in America, of Prescott, Bancroft, and Stephens; not a word of the companion of Bonomi, Robert Hay, and Wilkinson; the pioneer of Egyptology, the architect-draftsman of the Mosque of Omar, the panoramist of Leicester Square, the New York architect, the co-discoverer of the Mayan culture, the builder of South America's first railroad, the Argonaut of California. The New York newspapers, which over a period of fifteen years had printed many news releases on one of the greatest archaeological-explorers that ever lived did not once mention his name. That is until many days had passed and inquiries from remembering friends came to the editor of the *New York Herald*. Then, as a sort of afterthought, Catherwood appeared in a single line under 'The Saved and the Lost':

Mr. Catherwood Also is Missing

INTRODUCTION* TO VIEWS
OF ANCIENT MONUMENTS

The monuments represented in this Volume seem, from their novelty and peculiar character, to demand some preliminary explanations of the circumstances under which they are found to exist, and the historic interest that attaches to them, as the most important aids we possess, for the investigation of that great unsettled problem—the origin of the inhabitants of the American continent, and the sources from whence their early civilization was derived. No questions, merely antiquarian, have given rise to more earnest discussions than those involved in this subject; and, until of late years, the hardihood of the disputants has been in proportion to the scantiness of the evidence that had survived the ravages of conquest, and the iconoclastic bigotry of the earlier Christian missionaries. It is only within the present century that the attention of European scholars has been drawn to the fact, that a new and unexceptionable class of testimony, bearing directly on the Anti-Columbian History of the American continent, was within their reach; that there yet mouldered within the Forests of Yucatán and Guatemala, architectural and sculptural remains of vast size and mysterious purpose, still displaying (though yield-

---

* The author of *F. Catherwood, Archt* feels that this Introduction, written by Catherwood to preface his *Views*, should stand without any editorial additions, other than brief bracketed parentheses that will serve to explain Catherwood's text. It was written in 1844, when the published material on the Maya was no more than six volumes, and much of this fantastically inaccurate, and yet, Catherwood's, like the writings of Stephens and Prescott, has withstood the twin assault of time and archaeological investigation.

ing to a daily process of disintegration and decay) a high degree of constructive skill, and attesting, in their ornaments and proportions, to the prevalence of an indigenous and well established system of design, varying from any known models in the old world. The truth of this statement, though at first received with incredulity, has been satisfactorily established by later researches; and I may appeal to the following Drawings for its confirmation. They illustrate some of the more striking objects which engaged my notice as an Artist, during two expeditions, undertaken expressly with a view of exploring the ruined sites of Central America, and preserving some memorials of their present state. The first of these was devoted chiefly to the countries known under the above general title, including the States of Honduras, Guatemala, Chiapas, &c. The ruins at Copán and Palenque were visited during this journey, which occupied part of the years 1839 and 1840. A brief sojourn in Yucatán having shown the richness of the antiquarian harvest that there awaits the gleaner, a second journey, for its more thorough examination, was determined on, in the year 1841: in its progress most of the Drawings in the present Volume were made. The narrative of these expeditions will be found in the well-known works of Mr. J. L. Stephens, 'Incidents of Travel in Central America, Chiapas, and Yucatán,' 4 vols. 8vo., New York and London; to them, and to the lately published 'History of the Conquest of Mexico,' by Mr. Prescott, I must refer the reader desirous of further knowledge. In the one, he will meet with all the information that personal observation, directed by enterprise and enthusiasm, can supply; and in the other, all the light that a most extended range of research through the whole body of existing documentary evidence, can throw on the obscurity that shrouds the history of the unrecorded races— beyond the page of written annals—whose very existence we should be ignorant of, but for the contemplation of their colossal works, still before our eyes.

The term Central America is usually applied to the countries extending from the Republic of New Granada, on the south-west, to the boundaries of the great Mexican Confederation, on the north-east, from 8° to 18° of north latitude. They form the central portion of the long isthmus which unites North and South America, and divides the Atlantic Ocean from the Pacific, and are known as the States of Guatemala, St. Salvador, Honduras, Nicaragua, and Costa Rica. The peninsula of Yucatán, though politically distinct, is geographically connected with this region, and projects from its northern extremity into the Gulf of Mexico.

The natural characteristics of this district are as varied as its civil divisions. It may, however, be briefly described as an elevated table-land, broken at intervals by a central range of mountains, rising in some places to the height of six or seven thousand feet (which, by some geographers, is considered as the link connecting the chains of the Andes and the Rocky Mountains of the northern and southern continents), and which separates the waters that flow on either side to the Atlantic and Pacific Oceans. It is traversed in every direction by lateral ranges of hills, forming intermediate valleys, that extend to the coasts. The level of the country declines rapidly towards the sea-shores; they are generally low and swampy, and are intersected by lagoons. They teem with the rankest abundance of tropical vegetation, giving rise to fevers that prove fatally destructive to European constitutions. In many parts of Central America few settlements have been made by the Spanish conquerors, and large sections of it are still unvisited by strangers, and in possession of the independent Indian tribes.

The district allowed by the Spanish crown to the English, for the purposes of logwood cutting, occupies a portion of the sea-coast on the Bay of Honduras. From the unexplored and impracticable nature of the surrounding country, its boundaries have never been well defined; only a limited communication, liable to frequent interruptions, subsists between it and the adjoining Republics. The peninsula of Yucatán may be regarded as a continuation of the highland of Guatemala; it contains two regions, differing from each other in physical character. The southern part, as far as it has been visited by travellers and settlers of European origin, is found to contain vast tracts of alluvial soil, inundated during many months of the year by the swelling of its rivers in the rainy season, and rich in all the articles of tropical products. Here grow the immense forests of logwood and mahogany, from whence is drawn the chief supply of those articles for European consumption. Much of this district is apparently still unappropriated, or in the hands of the native Indians. A line drawn parallel to and between the 19th and 20th degrees of north latitude will describe the line of demarcation between this region and the northern half of the peninsula, where an entirely different conformation prevails. It has some remarkable physical features, and being the principal seat of the ancient remains delineated in this volume, has received more investigation than any of the neighboring countries. The division to the north of the above-mentioned line is composed of one mass of limestone, intermixed with silicious matter; its surface is slightly undulating, and, in a few places, rising into hills, which pierce through the stratum of vegetable mould that usually covers it. In the whole of this country there is neither river, rivulet, or spring.

Though the rains are very abundant in the rainy season, the soil absorbs the whole quantity which falls, and prevents the waters from uniting and forming water-courses or springs. In the depressions some water is collected in temporary ponds; they however are soon dried up. The remains of cisterns and reservoirs, intended to remedy this want, are among the most remarkable works that we find of the ancient inhabitants; from the decay of population they have mostly been neglected or abandoned, and the country would become unfit for the residence of man or beast, if it were not for the existence of an extraordinary species of natural wells, occurring as caverns in the limestone rock, and forming a succession of passages and chambers of very great depth, at the bottom of which are usually found sources of clear and pure water from ten to twenty feet deep. They are descended by rude ladders, and the whole supply of water has to be brought up by human labour from these subterranean recesses. One of the most singular that we met with, at Bolonchen, is drawn in Plate XX., which will give a better idea of these remarkable places than any description can do. The 'Senotes,' [*cenote*] as they are called, are large natural cavities in the rock, open to the sky, and water is found in them, at a depth of from twenty to one hundred feet from the level of the surrounding ground. The depth of the water is supposed to be very great. The limestone rocks supply excellent building materials, that have been equally made use of by the ancient and modern inhabitants. The Spanish towns are well and substantially built. The churches and monasteries everywhere display a solidity of structure, that bears witness to the enduring character of the religion and ecclesiastical polity imposed on the country by its conquerors. Owing to the secluded position of Yucatán, and its distance from the highways of commerce, the prevalent state of society has still much of primitive simplicity, and the two races inhabiting it are less distinct from one another in their social relations, than in the other countries once subject to Spain. The population of the towns is chiefly of Spanish extraction. The country is parcelled out in the possession of the great landholders, who spend the larger part of the year in the cities, occasionally visiting their country-houses, or Haciendas, which stand each in the centre of the surrounding domain, governed by a Major-domo, and encircled by the huts of the farm servants and their families. The mass of the rural population consists of a nation of aborigines, called in their own language Mayas, the undoubted descendants of the people who inhabited the country at the time of its discovery by Europeans. They retain few traces of the warlike tribes, who for twenty-five years withstood the attacks of the chivalry of Spain, and more than once drove the invaders from their shores. Three centuries of mild and unoppressive servitude has reduced them to the condition of agricultural labourers, mostly attached to the great estates by a species of feudal tenure, derived from the peculiar circumstances of the land. Where the natural wells above described are wanting, the large proprietors have constructed, at a great expense, on their estates, tanks and reservoirs to supply the deficiency of water, to obtain the use of which the Mayas are obliged to come under obligations of service to the owners. The Mayas have many points of personal resemblance with the North American Indians; they still retain their language—its structure has been investigated and explained by Spanish writers. Unfortunately for the antiquarian they are totally without historic traditions, nor is their curiosity excited by the presence of the monuments amongst which they live, to more than an indistinct feeling of religious romance and superstitious dread. The political history of Yucatán is told in a few words. From the time of the conquest it existed as a distinct captain-generalcy under the Spanish rule, and in such a state of isolation, that there is no record of its having been visited by an European traveller, from the time of the conquest until the present century. It so remained up to the era when the Mexican states acquired their independence, generally adhering to the government established in Mexico, and forming one of the States of the Mexican confederation. The Federal system of Mexico being superseded in 1835 by a Central government, the change excited discontent in Yucatán, and led to a succession of conflicts, which ended in the expulsion of the Mexicans in 1840. More lately the energies of Santa Anna have been employed in re-asserting the supremacy of Mexico, and from the latest accounts it appears that he has succeeded by negotiation in once more uniting Yucatán to that country.

The Ancient Monuments of Yucatán and Central America now claim our attention. In addition to the descriptions to each plate, I offer here a few general remarks, followed by a brief account of the principal places visited by Mr. Stephens and myself, and a sketch of the probable opinions as to their builders. The prevailing type of architecture which we are struck with throughout these regions, is the construction of immense artificial pyramidal mounds, or terraces, of greater or less height, not terminating in a point, like the Egyptian examples, but having, on their summits, platforms that support ponderous structures of hewn stone, unquestionably, in most instances, erected for purposes of a sacred character. Whether these mounds or pyramids are in general solid, or contain, in all cases, passages and apartments, is not ascertained. In the few that have been opened, by accident or design, small arched rooms have been found. The superincumbent buildings are generally long, low, arched, and of a single story in height—a style of building frequently adopted by the Spaniards, on account of the shocks of earthquakes to which many parts of the country are exposed. In a few instances, buildings of two or three stories have been met with. These 'Teocalli,' or 'Houses of God' (as they are still called by the Indians), abound in every part of Yucatán. In front of the temples the statues of their deities were formerly seen conspicuous; and the sacrificial stone, convex on its upper surface, so as to raise the chest of the human victim, has not in all cases disappeared.

The following account of the Mexican temples and religious sacrifices, from Prescott's 'History of the Conquest of Mexico,' possesses great interest, as shewing the identity of the religious usages of the ancient inhabitants of the two neighbouring states; and derives confirmation from a comparison with the remains in Yucatán, scarcely any vestiges of such buildings now existing in

Mexico Proper, owing, no doubt, to its being more directly the seat of the Spanish sway.

The Mexican temples were called 'Teocalli,' or 'Houses of God,' and were very numerous. There were several hundreds in each of the principal cities, many of them, doubtless, very humble edifices. They were solid masses of earth, brick, or stone, and in their form somewhat resembled the pyramidal structures of Ancient Egypt. The bases of many of them were several hundred feet square, and they towered to a height of more than a hundred feet. They had staircases leading from the base to the summit, on which stood the temple with altars, on which fires were kept, as inextinguishable as those in the Temple of Vesta. There were said to be six hundred of these altars, on smaller buildings, within the enclosure of the great Temple of Mexico, which, with those on the sacred edifices in other parts of the city, shed a brilliant illumination over its streets through the darkest night. From the construction of their temples, all religious services were public. The long processions ascending their massive sides, as they rose higher and higher towards the summit, and the dismal rites of the sacrifice performed there, were all visible from the remotest corners of the capital, impressing on the spectator's mind a superstitious veneration for the mysteries of his religion, and for the dread ministers by whom they were interpreted. Human sacrifices were adopted by the Aztecs, or Mexicans, early in the 14th century, about two hundred years before the conquest of Mexico. Rare at first, they became more frequent with the wider extent of their empire, till at length almost every festival was closed with this cruel abomination. One of their most important festivals was that in honour of the god Tezcatlipoca, whose rank was inferior only to that of the Supreme Being. He was called 'the soul of the world,' and supposed to have been its creator. He was depicted as a handsome man, endowed with perpetual youth. A year before

126

the intended sacrifice, a captive, distinguished for his personal beauty, and without a blemish on his body, was selected to represent this deity. Certain tutors took charge of him, and instructed him how to perform his new part with becoming grace and dignity. He was arrayed in a splendid dress, regaled with incense, and with a profusion of sweet-scented flowers. When he went abroad he was attended by a train of the royal pages, and as he halted in the streets to play some favourite melody, the crowd prostrated themselves before him, and did him homage, as the representative of their good deity. In this way he lived an easy, luxurious life, feasted at the banquets of the principal nobles, who paid him all the honours of a divinity.

At length the fatal day of sacrifice arrived. The term of his short-lived glories was at an end. He was stripped of his gaudy apparel, and conducted in one of the royal barges across the lake, which surrounded the capital, to a temple which rose on its margin, about a league distant. Hither the inhabitants of the capital flocked to witness the consummation of the ceremony. As the procession ascended the sides of the pyramid, the unhappy victim threw away his gay chaplet of flowers, and broke in pieces the musical instruments with which he had solaced the hours of captivity. On the summit he was received by six priests, whose long and matted locks flowed disorderly over their sable robes, covered with hieroglyphical scrolls of mystic import. They led him to the sacrificial stone, a huge block of jasper, with its upper surface somewhat convex. On this the prisoner was stretched. Five priests secured his head and his limbs, while the sixth, clad in a scarlet mantle, emblematic of his bloody office, dexterously opened the breast of the wretched victim with a sharp razor of *itzli*,—a volcanic substance, hard as flint,—and inserting his hand in the wound, tore out the palpitating heart. The minister of death, first holding this up towards the sun, an object of worship to the Mexicans, cast it at the feet of the deity to whom the temple was devoted, while the multitudes below prostrated themselves in humble adoration. The tragic story of this prisoner was expounded by the priests as the type of human destiny, which, brilliant in its commencement, too often

127

closes in sorrow and disaster. The most loathsome part of the story—the manner in which the body of the sacrificed victim was disposed of—remains yet to be told. It was delivered to the warrior who had taken him in battle, and by him, after being dressed, was served up in an entertainment to his friends. This was not the coarse repast of famished cannibals, but a banquet, teeming with all the docorum of civilized life. It is stated that, in some years, twenty thousand captives were offered in sacrifice to their deities.

We thus see the dreadful purposes to which these edifices were applied, and I think there can be but one opinion as to the altars, idols, and sacrificial stones at Quirigua and Copán having been constructed and used for these dismal rites. Indeed, the channels cut on the upper surfaces of the sacrificial stones is quite conclusive on my mind as to this fact.

Another, and not less distinguishing, feature than their mounds or pyramids, are the arched rooms found in almost all the ancient buildings. I call it an arch, [corbeled arch] because it has all the appearance of one, and answers most of its purposes, and the inventors were on the very threshold of discovering the true principles of the arch. It invariably consists of stones overlaying each other from opposite walls, until the last meet over the centre of the room; or, what is still more commonly the case, when the last stones approach within about twelve inches of each other, a flat stone is laid on the top, covered either with solid masonry or concrete. The joints of the stones are all horizontal. The roofs have a slight inclination, to throw off the rain, and are cemented. This form of arch appears at first sight original, and is so, inasmuch as regards the Indians; but the same principle was used in the earliest times by the Egyptians, the Greeks, and the Etrurians, and would, in all probability, suggest itself to any people who had to construct a stone roof over a space too wide for them to cover with flat stones.

We are not enabled to discriminate with any degree of certainty the original purpose of the remaining classes of ancient buildings. It is impossible to doubt, however, that some of these— as, for example, the Palace at Palenque (Plate VI.)—were intended for the chosen seats of the political and hierarchal authorities. They still (amidst ruin and neglect) show their adaptation for those great exhibitions of barbaric pomp and splendour, the occurrence of which is noticed in all the relations of the Spanish discoverers. Others, as Las Monjas, and the Casa del Gobernador, at Uxmal (Plates VIII. and X.), seem constructed for the residence of ecclesiastical communities not unlike the monastic societies of the Old World), to whom was delegated the performance of the ritual worship of the gods, and whose influence extended through the entire framework of social life. The monolithic idols at Copán may, with much probability, be referred to a period anterior to that of the Aztec domination, and have some characteristics that appear to connect them with a prior race, either the mysterious Toltecs, whose disappearance from Mexico took place within the range of historic record, and who spread themselves over the regions of Central America, or the still earlier people whose country they occupied in their migrations. One of the most singular facts attending the consideration of the arts of the people by whom these buildings were erected, is the certainty that they were unacquainted with the use of iron; this is expressly asserted by the Spaniards, and we find no reason to doubt its truth. Masses of meteoric iron, indeed, are met with in all parts of the American continent; but the natives were ignorant of the process of working this metal, and, in lieu of it, used copper instruments, hardened by the admixture of tin, or some other alloy.* Their buildings of stone, and sculptures in granite, were worked with copper tools; and besides having a perfect knowledge of the processes of stone-cutting and laying, they were well acquainted with various kinds of mortars, stuccoes, and cements, and large masses of excellent

---

* Here Catherwood is mistaken. The Mayas used only stone celts as tools.

'concrete,' as it is technically termed, are found in many of their buildings; they were, in fact, so far as regards the mechanical part, accomplished masons. In another department of the arts, indicating a higher degree of civilization than that exhibited in the erection of pyramids and temples, they had made a remarkable advance. I allude to the art of painting, and the preparation, mixing, and use of pigments. Their painting is, indeed, superior to their architecture and sculpture: like the same art amongst the ancient Egyptians, it was applied for purposes of architectural decoration. In the blending of various colours, they had attained a step beyond the practice of that nation, approaching more nearly to the less severe style of art found in the frescoes of Pompeii and Herculaneum. Such an assertion may seem to need some corroborative proof: I regret that it is not at present in my power to offer any. These remains, from the very fragility of their nature, have, in too many cases, utterly perished. In one place only, at Chichén Itza, were we gratified with the discovery of large specimens of them, though it is probable that they formed part of the ornaments of every building of consequence when in a perfect state. At this spot, where of all others I desired the full possession of health and strength, I was incapacitated by severe illness and fever from delineating them, and was obliged to leave these most interesting objects to the mercy of accident and wanton outrage, to which they may before this time have fallen victims.

I should mention, however, that in one of the rooms of a large building at Chichén Itza, are paintings covering the entire walls, from the floor to the ceiling. The apartment (I speak from recollection) may be twenty-five feet long, ten feet wide, and fifteen feet high. The figures are not more than six to eight inches in height; but most interesting subjects are represented, abounding with life, animation, and nature. In one place are seen warriors preparing for battle; in another the fight is at its height: castles

130

are attacked, defended, and taken, and various military punishments follow. This forms one section of the wall. In another are labours of husbandry—planting, sowing, and reaping; and the cultivation of fruits and flowers. Then follow domestic scenes, and others apparently of a mythological nature; indeed, almost everything requisite to give us an intimate acquaintance with Indian life is depicted. The subjects are too numerous to mention, and such was the multitude of figures and objects, that a month would not have sufficed for copying them, and they gave me a much higher opinion of the state of civilization among the Indians than I had previously entertained. Unfortunately, these beautiful specimens of art are fast hastening to decay, and every day adds to their approaching obliteration.

I will now give a brief outline of the chief points of interest visited by Mr. Stephens and myself.

The first place we attempted to reach was Copán, in the state of Honduras, to which our attention had been drawn by the account of the late Colonel Galindo, a Spanish officer, in the service of the Republic of Central America. We sought in vain for information until we arrived at Gualan, within fifty miles of it. The Padre, or Catholic priest, had been there many years before, but his accounts were so improbable, and evidently drawn so much from a lively imagination, that we much doubted whether it were worth while to go there at all. By a singular perversion of this gentleman's mind, or by a sad defect in his memory, he minutely described things which could not exist, and never mentioned a single one of the many curious objects that meet the traveller's gaze on wandering over the ruins of this city. When arrived almost within sight of them, we had unforeseen difficulties to encounter; for some time no guide could be found, and at the only house where we could be lodged (there being no inns in the country), we were inhospitably received. To the praise of

the Spaniards, be it said, it was the only instance of the kind we
met with in our long journey. Mr. Stephens very truly remarks,
'Don Gregorio's house had two sides to it, an inside and an out,'
to which latter he graciously gave us free access, by securely
bolting his door, on retiring, to rest, and then wishing us good
night. I mention this circumstance to show the difficulties travellers may meet with in visiting these countries, and the perseverance
necessary to overcome them.

Copán may be called the City of Idols, as it abounds with
monolithic statues of Indian deities. It stands on the bank of a
river, and was surrounded by walls; that on the riverside is still,
in places, from sixty to ninety feet in height. The remains of a
vast temple, or collection of sacred edifices, lie scattered about,
together with innumerable fragments of mutilated ornaments and
statues. The most remarkable of the idols are delineated in Plates I.,
III., IV., and V. They are about twelve feet in height and four
feet square; the front and back being, in general, representations
of human figures, habited in a most singular manner, with towering head-dresses of feathers and skins of animals, the necks
adorned with necklaces, the ears with ear-rings, and the feet with
sandals, like those of the ancient Romans. The sides are carved
with hieroglyphics, which no one has yet been able to decipher.*
They were all painted. There are no remains of arched buildings
here, though no doubt such formerly existed; but immense pyramidal mounds and terraced walls are met with to a great distance

---

* Since Catherwood's time, considerable progress has been made on the deciphering of Maya glyphs. The discovery of Bishop Diego de Landa's *Historia de
las cosas de Yucatán* (written about 1566) and published by Brasseur de Bourbourg in 1865, while it did not prove to be a 'Rosetta Stone,' nonetheless, was
the first step in the unraveling of the glyph puzzle. The Maya inscriptions, as
Dr. Morley explained 'treat primarily of chronology, astronomy and religious
matters'; they are in no sense records of personal glorification. As the deciphering
stands now about forty per cent of the known corpus of Maya inscriptions has
been, more or less, deciphered; the rest, as in Catherwood's time, remains a blank.
See *The Ancient Maya* by Sylvanus G. Morley, chap. 12, 'Hieroglyphic
Writing, Arithmetic and Astronomy.' Palo Alto, 1946.

in the surrounding forests. If the intelligent Padre of Gualan dealt in the marvellous, it is not surprising that the ignorant Indians went far beyond him; I heard wonderful accounts of the Cave of Tibulco, but all my efforts to reach this abode of the genii were unavailing.

Quirigua is the next place of interest in this part of the country; but we did not hear of it for some weeks after our arrival. It is within six miles of the high road we had passed in going to Gualan, and yet, with all our inquiries for ruined cities, no one seemed to be acquainted with it. It is in many respects similar to Copán, but probably more ancient.* It consists of ruined mounds and terraces, with many colossal statues, deeply buried in the entanglement of a tropical forest. Some of the statues are twenty-six feet in height, of a single stone; the sculpture is in lower relief than at Copán; and, as usual, there are numerous hieroglyphics. I regretted exceedingly not being able to make other than slight sketches of these remarkable monuments; but I was alone, and the difficulties were too great to be overcome single-handed. In order to reach the ruins, I had to descend a rapid and dangerous river in a small ricketty canoe, and then cut a path for a mile, through a forest, such as none can fully understand who have not been in a tropical country. The distance which, in descending the river, was performed in an hour, required four in ascending; so that the greater part of the day was taken up in going and returning.

At Santa Cruz Del Quiche, are ruins of vast extent, but so dilapidated, that little remains for the draughtsman. It was here that we first heard of the mysterious Indian city, still existing in all its Pagan splendour, in the midst of a country not yet visited

---

* Quirigua, as Catherwood deduced, 'is in many respects similar to Copán,' although it is not older than Copán. It was formed as a colony from the older city-state of Copán.

by white man. We were strongly tempted to try the adventure, but prudential motives, and the advanced state of the season, prevented us. From subsequent inquiries, in distant parts of the country, I have little doubt but that such a city exists, but the danger of reaching it would be great.*

At Ocasingo, we met with the arch before alluded to, with the usual accompaniments of mounds and terraces, and an ornament over one of the doorways, not unlike the winged globe of Egypt.

Palenque, in Chiapas, the most southern province of Mexico, is better known than any other of the ruined American cities: my notice of it will therefore be short. It was probably abandoned, and in ruins, when Cortes passed near it, in his celebrated march from Mexico to Honduras,† as no mention is made of it in his despatches. The principal building is (with reason, I think) called the Palace. It stands on an artificial mound, whose base is three hundred and ten feet by two hundred and sixty feet, and forty feet high, with staircases on the four sides. The building itself measures two hundred and twenty-eight feet by one hundred and eighty feet, twenty-five feet high, and is of one story. The front and rear have each fourteen doorways, and eleven on each end. The piers dividing the doorways still present traces of admirable stuccoes, which were painted. The interior is divided into three courtyards, with a tower in one of them. Every part appears to have been elaborately decorated with sculpture in stone, stuccoes, and paintings. In several of the apartments, which have the usual triangular arch, I noticed that the walls had been painted

---

* This 'white mysterious city, inhabited by Indians' was a famous hoax of the period; the ruined cities were there and were later discovered in numerous places in the forested area of El Peten. The hoax of the inhabited city was taken up by P. T. Barnum who exhibited a dwarf 'Aztec Princess' which he vowed was captured in this mysterious city of El Peten. See p. 71.

† Palenque was abandoned in the 8th century long before Cortes made his famous march into Honduras (1524).

several times, as traces of earlier subjects were discernible where the outer coat of paint had been destroyed. The paintings were of the same nature as the frescoes of Italy,—water-colours applied to cement. The other buildings are inferior in size to the Palace, but all on high mounds, richly decorated with numerous stone tablets of hieroglyphics, and sculptures of figures well executed, which have awakened a lively interest in the antiquarian world. The whole is shrouded in the depths of a tropical forest, which has to be cleared away at every fresh visit of the traveller. Casts were made of the most interesting sculptures, which were subsequently seized by the agents of the Mexican government, and are doubtless ere this destroyed. Plates VI. and VII. will assist the reader in obtaining an idea of this remarkable place.

We now come to the ruins of Uxmal, in Yucatán, which, for their vast extent, their variety, and being for the most part in good preservation, may claim precedence in this Province of any other remains of antiquity. They impressed my mind at the first glance with the same feelings of wonder and admiration, with which I first caught sight of the ruins of Thebes. I will not institute a comparison between Uxmal and the 'World's great Empress on the Egyptian Plain,' but still the several Teocalli, rising higher than any buildings at Thebes—the gigantic terraces supporting immense and solid structures of stone—the vast amount of sculptured decorations, and the novelty and intricacy of the designs—all tend to impress the beholder with sentiments of awe and admiration.

The 'Casa de las Monjas,' or House of the Nuns, is a building forming four sides of a square, and inclosing a courtyard, about three hundred feet each way. Each of the four buildings shows a different design, so also do the rear fronts and the ends, presenting no less than sixteen different façades. All were richly decorated and painted; their present appearance is represented in the Plates

XIV. and XV. From these a judgment may be formed of the entire building when in a perfect state, each ornament and moulding relieved by rich and vivid colours, and portions probably gilt. The effect must have been gorgeous in the extreme.

The grand Teocallis, called by the Indians the 'House of the Diviner,' stood to the eastward of the last-mentioned building, and within a hundred yards of it. The pyramidal part rose to the height of a hundred feet above the plain, with two noble flights of stairs leading to the platform on the top. Here stood the building represented in the Plates XI. and XII., and I will not attempt to explain by words what is better understood from inspecting the design: viewed from all parts, this edifice was singularly beautiful and graceful.

The 'Casa del Gobernador,' or House of the Governor, is next in importance. This immense building is constructed entirely of hewn stone, and measures three hundred and twenty feet in front, by forty feet in depth; the height is about twenty-six feet. It has eleven doorways in front, and one at each end. The apartments are narrow, seldom exceeding twelve feet, just large enough to swing a hammock, which was, and still is, the substitute for beds throughout the country. Some of the rooms are long, measuring sixty feet, and twenty-three feet high. There does not appear to have been any internal decoration, nor are there any windows. The lower part of the edifice is of plain wrought stone, but the upper part is singularly rich in ornament, as delineated in Plates IX. and X. Taking the front, the ends, and the rear of the building, we have a length of seven hundred and fifty-two feet of elaborate carving, on which traces of painting are still visible. The peculiar arch of the country has been employed in every room. The lintels of the doorways were of wood, a more costly but less durable material than stone, and from its hardness more difficult to be worked.

Unfortunately they have all decayed, and the masonry they supported has fallen down, and much of the beauty of the building is thus destroyed. The Casa del Gobernador stands on three terraces; the lowest is three feet high, fifteen feet wide, and five hundred and seventy-five feet long; the second is twenty feet high, two hundred and fifty feet wide, and five hundred and forty-five feet long; and the third is nineteen feet high, thirty feet broad, and three hundred and sixty feet long. They are all of stone, and in a tolerable state of preservation. These are the principal buildings at Uxmal, and the others are much inferior in size and condition.

We found at Kabah, in addition to richly-decorated façades, some very curious specimens of internal decoration (see Plate XVII.); at Zayi, [Zayil] an immense edifice, of three stories in height; at Labnah, a handsome gateway, of which a drawing will be found at Plate XIX.; at Bolonchen, a natural curiosity in a deep subterranean well, the descent to which is by long ranges of ladders, of dangerous construction (see Plate XX.); at Chichén Itza, ruins little inferior in extent or interest to those of Uxmal (a drawing of a façade of one of the buildings is given in Plate XXI.); at Tuloom, [Tulum] a walled city, of which there are two drawings (Plates XXIII. and XXIV.); at Izamal,* some large mounds and a colossal head (Plate XXV); and, finally, at Aké, a collection of large stones on a high mound, not unlike a Druidical monument.

It is impossible to survey the monuments now described without feeling some curiosity respecting the people by whom they were built, and the state of society which led to their erection. Nor has the question been unproductive of discussion, though hitherto a desire to theorise has preceded a complete and accurate

---

* This stone face at Izamal as been wholly destroyed. The only record of it is Catherwood's drawing.

survey of the monuments themselves, from whence the only safe foundations for theory can be derived. Two circumstances may be noted in all the writers who have made researches on this topic—a general, and, perhaps, natural, wish to carry their antiquity up to a very early period and a constant effort to connect them, in any possible way, with the history and traditions of the Old World. Thus, the work of Lord Kingsborough (unquestionably the most splendid example of private munificence ever applied to the promotion of antiquarian literature) appears to owe its origin chiefly to the author's conviction in the truth of his favourite hypothesis,—the colonisation of America by the lost tribes of Israel. Other writers have even attributed them to an antediluvian period. Waldeck, a careful explorer of these ruins, infers, from the growth of trees and the accumulation of vegetable soil in some of the court-yards at Palenque, that they cannot be less than from two thousand to three thousand years old. My own observations have led me to differ from these conclusions, and to consider them as founded on insufficient data.

The growth of tropical trees has not been sufficiently studied to make them a safe criterion to judge of the age of monuments; and the only trees of large dimensions I met with, were those of quick growth; one, in the village of Ticul, of six feet diameter, having attained that size in thirty years, as I was informed by the person who planted it. I am, moreover, inclined to the opinion that very ancient trees are not to be met with in tropical latitudes; and that rapid decay generally, or always, accompanies rapid growth. The accumulation of vegetable mould to the depth of nine feet, is another proof that has been adduced in favour of the high antiquity of the buildings where it occurs; and, doubtless, in a northern climate, it would indicate a remote age, but not so in the tropics; vegetation there is so rank and rapid, that within less than twelve months from our first visit to Uxmal, we found the whole place so overgrown with shrubs and small trees, that nothing but the high teocalli and the outline of the other monuments were visible, and a thick deposit of vegetable mould covered the places we had so short a time before cleared away. I have met with no physical marks, surely indicating a high antiquity; on the contrary, the whole course of my observations have led me to form an opposite opinion. It is true there are misshapen mounds, so utterly destroyed that they might belong to any time or any people; but I have little doubt that excavations would prove them to have been built by cognate races to those who inhabited the country at the time of the conquest. It is also proved, by undoubted testimony, that many of the buildings we now see in ruins, were in use by the Indians at the time of the Spanish invasion. I do not think we should be safe in ascribing to any of the monuments (which still retain their form) a greater age than from eight hundred to one thousand years; * and those which are perfect enough to be delineated, I think it likely are not more than from four to six hundred years old. The roots of trees and the tropical rains are the chief elements of destruction, and daily and hourly is the work going on. Another century will hardly have elapsed, before the whole of these interesting monuments will have become indistinguishable heaps of ruins.

With regard to the various theories that have been formed to trace the nations that peopled the American continent, through their migrations, to their original habitation in the Old World, we find them all resting for support upon a few vague similarities of rites and customs, more or less common amongst every branch of the human family. Besides, the idea that civilisation, and its at-

---

* This deduction of Uxmal's time-period is most remarkable, for flying in the face of the learned antiquarians of the period that gave it great antiquity, Catherwood put the buildings within the range of history. We know now that Uxmal, part of the League of Mayapan was founded by the Maya leader Ah Zuitol Tutul Xiu between 987-1007 A.D., which puts it within Catherwood's first estimate of its being 'from eight hundred to one thousand years' old.

tendant arts, is in every case *derivative*, and always owing to a
transmission from a cultivated to an unpolished people, is eminently unphilosophical, as it only removes further back, without
explaining the original difficulty of *invention*, which must somewhere have taken place; and if at any time in one country, undoubtedly a similar train of circumstances may have led to
similar results in another. The latest writer on this subject (Mr.
Prescott) has come to the conclusion, after a dispassionate and
unprejudiced view of the existing evidence, that though 'the
coincidences are sufficiently strong to authorize a belief that the
civilisation of Anahuac (ancient Mexico) was in some degree in-
fluenced by Eastern Asia, yet the discrepancies are so great as to
carry back the communication to a very remote period, so remote,
that this foreign influence has been too feeble to interfere materi-
ally with the growth of what may be regarded, in its essential
features, as a peculiar and indigenous civilisation.' The results
arrived at by Mr. Stephens and myself, after a full and precise
comparative survey of the ancient remains, coincide with this
opinion, and are briefly:—that they are not of immemorial antiquity, the work of unknown races; but that, as we now see them,
they were occupied, and possibly erected, by the Indian tribes
in possession of the country at the time of the Spanish conquest,—
that they are the production of an indigenous school of art, adapted
to the natural circumstances of the country, and to the civil and
religious polity then prevailing,—and that they present but very
slight and accidental analogies with the works of any people or
country in the Old World. The reader will find the general
argument ably treated in the 'Incidents of Travel in Yucatán,'
Vol. II. I will content myself with a few illustrative remarks.

1st. These buildings coincide, in the minutest particulars,
with the descriptions of the old Spanish historians, and contemporary chroniclers of the conquest, who speak with wonder and

astonishment of the stately stone buildings that met their eyes in their progress through the country; and we often read of them in connection with commendations bestowed on the praiseworthy zeal which caused their devastation, and the almost entire destruction of all traces of Mexican civilisation. So completely was this effected, that we find the historian, Robertson, writing—'At this day there does not remain the smallest vestige of any Indian building, public or private, in Mexico, or any province of New Spain.' The fallacy of this assertion is too obvious to need remark; coming from a respectable source, it gained credence, and has tended to needlessly obscure the true facts.

2nd. The architectural remains in Yucatán testify to the existence of a state of society, which, from other sources, we know to have prevailed in the neighbouring countries. Reasoning, *a priori*, from a survey of these ruins, and putting out of view the historical information at your command, it is obvious,—that, in the construction of these stupendous works, at a period when the mechanical resources for facilitating labour were imperfectly known, immense numbers of artisans must have been employed,—that these works are not of apparent utility, or such as would suggest themselves to the spontaneous and undirected energies of a nation, but that there must have existed a supreme, and probably despotic power, with authority sufficient to wield and direct the exertions of a subordinate population to purposes subservient to the display of civil or religious pomp and splendour,—that, for the sustenance of masses of people thus brought in contact, a certain progress must have been attained in the agricultural and economic sciences,—that many experiments must have failed, and many attempts been made, before the degree of proficiency in building, sculpture, and painting, which we now see, was reached,—and that, in a country where only the rudest means of transmitting knowledge from one generation to another was employed, it is probable the traditionary facts acquired by experience would be preserved by a sacred caste or tribe of priests, by whom, and for whose use, many of these buildings were undoubtedly erected. All these circumstances (and the same train of reasoning might be pursued to a much greater extent), existed in the civilisation of ancient Mexico. They were found by the Spaniards a numerous and thickly settled people, in possession of all the necessaries, and many of the comforts, of life, governed with absolute power by their king or cazique, and subject to the domination of a powerful hierarchy,—the sole depositories of scientific knowledge, and pervading with their influence every relation of social life.

3rd. Architectually considered, the ancient buildings of Yucatán show many features which imply an aboriginal character, derived from an imitation of natural objects. In Herrera's 'Account of Yucatán' we find it remarked, 'that there were so many and such stately stone buildings that it was amazing, and the greatest wonder was that, having no use of any metal, they were able to raise such structures, which seem to have been temples, for their houses were all of timber and thatched.' This original style of house (in use, no doubt, from the earliest period, and still found exclusively in Indian villages,—the walls constructed of bamboo canes, or trunks of trees, placed upright, and bound together by withes, with lattice-work apertures for windows, and an over-hanging, heavily-thatched roof), seems to have been the prototype * of much that we find peculiar among the ornamental architectural work of the country. If the Vitruvian theory, by which the characteristic forms of the early Grecian temples are traced to the influence of their original timber construction, be

---

* In this, too, Catherwood is borne out by the latest researches; the 'overhanging, heavily-thatched roof' was the prototype of Maya architecture. As in the Greek or Roman, the wooden house was projected into stone buildings; thus the Maya. The thatched hut of the Maya Indian became the model of the Maya corbel-arched stone buildings.

correct, a similar inference may fairly be drawn in this instance. The peculiarities of imitation are most evident in the plainer (and, no doubt, earlier) buildings; these, as less generally interesting, are not included in the illustrations of the present work. A reference to the plates of the second volume of Stephens' 'Incidents of Travel in Yucatán,' which represent the ruins of Chunhuhu, Kewick, Sabachtsche, Zayi, [Zayil] and many others, will show more clearly than the most laboured description, the fact that is now stated.

4th. The old Spanish and native historians inform us, that a nation, called the Toltecs, coming from the north, entered and took possession of the great valley in which the city of Mexico stands, about the close of the seventh century. We shall for ever remain in ignorance of the history of this people (except from such slight accounts and traditions as have come down to us through their successors, the Mexicans), unless we succeed in deciphering the hieroglyphic writing found at Palenque, Copán, and other places; and which seem to indicate an advance beyond the mere picture-writing of the Mexicans, being evidently compound characters, formed by abbreviation of the original pictorial signs, like the Chinese characters at the present day. The Mexicans described the Toltecs to the Spanish conquerors as having been well acquainted with agriculture, the mechanic arts, and working in metals. After holding sway for four hundred years, they disappeared before the more ferocious Aztecs, or Mexicans, who are said to have come from the northwest. The Toltecs, it is supposed, went to the south and east, taking possession of Central America and Yucatán, entering the latter by way of Honduras and Bacalar, first founding the cities of Quirigua and Copán.* The period when

---

* The Toltecs did not build Quirigua or Copán; this was accomplished in the time of the Old Empire and was pure Maya in concept, the Toltecs then did not have their rise.

143

they entered Yucatán is not known, nor am I inclined to place much reliance on the dates before-mentioned. At all events, it is probable that the Toltecs and their descendants erected the buildings we have been considering; and the Mexicans, or Aztecs,* adopted the arts and civilisation of their predecessors, used the same method of astronomical calculation, and were probably, in all essential peculiarities, a kindred race.

---

* In this deduction Catherwood is correct. The Toltecs did invade the coastal section of Yucatán between the years 1190-1441, bringing with them the Mexican cult of Quetzalcoatl, which became among the Maya 'Kulkulkhan'; its motif was introduced into the architecture.

VIEWS

OF

ANCIENT MONVMENTS

IN

CENTRAL AMERICA

CHIAPAS

AND

YVCATAN

BY

F. CATHERWOOD, ARCH.ᵀ

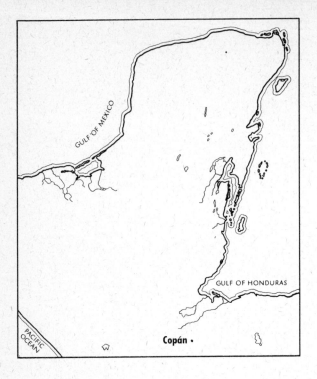

Plate I *Idol at Copán (Honduras).* A Maya time-marker erected every hotun (1800 days) as a form of five-year almanac, describing in the glyphs that cover its sides and back the principal astronomical and, perhaps, historical events of the preceding five-year period. There are thirteen steles in the Great Plaza at Copán, each carved from a single piece of limestone quarried from the hills near by and rolled down to its place in the Great Plaza. This sculpture measures 11 ft. 8 in. high, 3 ft. 4 in. square, and rests on a stone podium 6 ft. square. This is Stele H, carved and set up 4 Ahau 18 Muan, *c.* A. D. 782. The original drawing is in the Peabody Museum, Harvard University.

Lithographed by Andrew Picken.

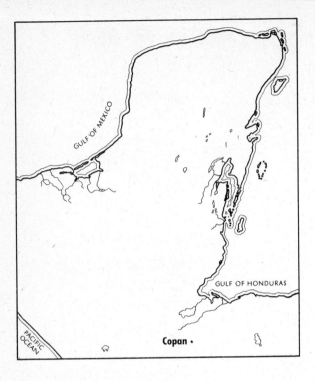

GULF OF MEXICO

GULF OF HONDURAS

PACIFIC OCEAN

Copan ·

Plate II *Pyramidal Building and Fragments of Sculpture at Copán (Honduras)*. View of a section of the Great Hieroglyphic Stairway, built about A. D. 766. The stairway with its two thousand glyphs had tumbled down in a mass of carved rubble long before the visit of Frederick Catherwood and John L. Stephens. In this view, Catherwood attempts to perform a synthesis of the Copánec carvings. In the foreground, a large sacrificial stone; to the right, a Maya head framed in the open mouth of a snake, which is part of the Hieroglyphic Stairway. The monkeys are apocryphal. Although there were two species of monkeys at Copán during their visit — Capuchins and Spider monkeys — these drawn by Catherwood are African Rhesus monkeys.

Lithographed by Henry Warren.

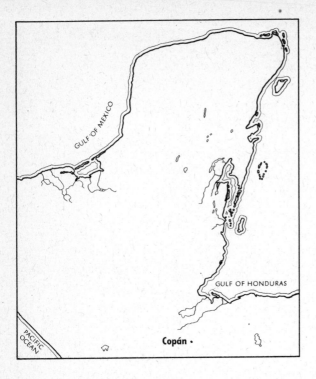

GULF OF MEXICO

GULF OF HONDURAS

PACIFIC OCEAN

Copán •

Plate III *Back of an Idol at Copán (Honduras)*. The glyphic inscriptions of Stele F are a superb piece of carving in low relief. The glyphs are enclosed in a twisted-rope motif, and the sides ornamented with a mimicry of quetzal plumes. Originally the stele was painted in violent polychromy. Catherwood's delineation of the glyphs is so accurate that modern archaeologists can read the inscription. Stele F, probably set up in the middle of the seventh century, has the Maya dates of 4 Ahau Chen. The original drawing is in the Peabody Museum, Harvard University.

Lithographed by Henry Warren.

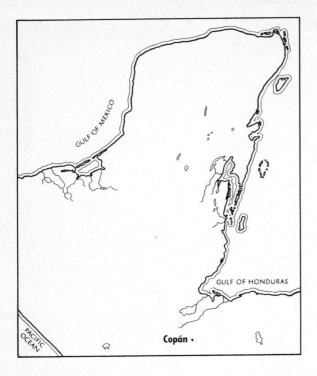

Plate IV *Broken Idol at Copán (Honduras)*. Stele C, broken by an earth tremor centuries ago, lies on its side near a large naturalistic lava-stone tortoise. Stele C, with the Maya dates of 12 Ahau 13 Kayab, probably erected *c.* A. D. 652, is one of the most beautiful of Maya carvings in the round, 'and in workmanship,' writes Catherwood, 'is equal to the best remains of Egyptian art. Its present condition [in 1839] may give some idea of the scene of desolation and ruin presented at Copán.' The ruins of Copán have now been restored by the Carnegie Institution of Washington. The original sepia is owned by Henry Schnackenberg, Esq., Newton, Conn.

Lithographed by Henry Warren.

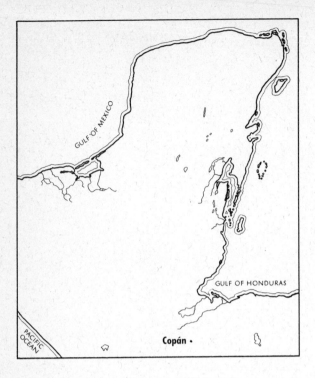

Plate V *Idol and Altar at Copán (Honduras)*. Built at the extreme eastern end of the 850-foot-long Great Plaza, it rests at the base of a short pyramid of steps — somewhat exaggerated in Catherwood's drawing. The zoomorphic altar, 3 ft. 6 in. high, measuring 7 ft. from angle to angle, is sculptured in the form of four enormous heads with horrendous fangs and protruding eyes. Channels on its flat top carried off the blood of sacrificial victims. The stone still carries something of its color. Stele D, which dominates it, was carved out of monolithic limestone, 11 ft. 9 in. high, 3 ft. square. Its sides and back are covered with glyphs and a Maya date, 10 Chuen, 8 Chen, *c.* A. D. 652.

Lithographed by William Parrott.

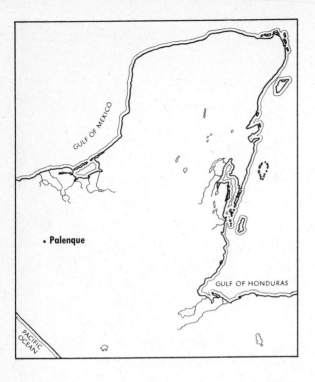

Plate VI *General View of Palenque (Chiapas, Mexico)*. One of the last cities of the Old Maya Empire to be erected, Palenque is situated in Chiapas, Mexico — bordering Guatemala — and set in the Tumbala hills. The Maya architects placed it at the end of a deep gorge flanked on three of its sides by towering verdured hills. A little less than one thousand feet above sea level, Palenque is intensely tropical. Drawn from a number of different sketches — for the ruins were jungle-covered and offered no panorama — as Catherwood freely admits, this lithograph shows the principal Palenquean buildings: the Palacio, to the extreme right, enclosing four sunken courts that fashion it into an architectural complex; the Temples of the Sun, the Cross, and the Foliated Cross; all stand on high pyramids — dramatized in the illustrations. Palenque was occupied during the seventh and eighth centuries. It is now being restored by the archaeologists of the Republic of Mexico.

Lithographed by Andrew Picken.

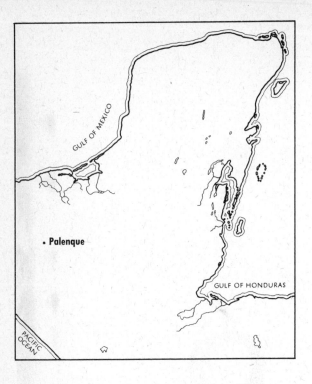

GULF OF MEXICO

GULF OF HONDURAS

PACIFIC OCEAN

• Palenque

Plate VII *(Upper)   Principal Court of the Palace at Palenque (Chiapas, Mexico).* The principal court of the Palacio rests on a truncated pyramid 30 ft. high. The building, constructed of rubble and faced with stucco, is approximately 225 ft. square and dominated by what was once a tall square tower — a very unusual Maya architectural feature. This illustration shows the west face of structure of the principal court with its nine large life-size figures carved in low relief.

(Lower)
The Interior of Casa, No. III (Temple of the Sun). An attempt is made by Catherwood to show the corbel arch used by the Maya architect, called by him 'Casa No. III' in his description. It was here in this Temple that Catherwood drew the famous 'Sun' relief, illustrated in this book.

Lithographed by Henry Warren.

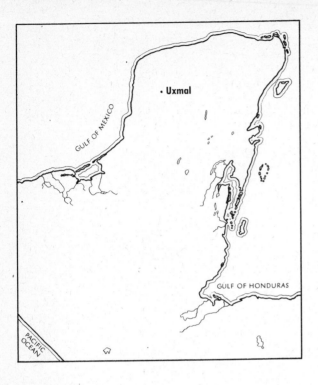

Plate VIII *General View of Las Monjas, Uxmal (Yucatán)*.
Uxmal, one of the principal cities of the League of Mayapán,
lies 45 miles to the southwest of Merida, capital of Yucatán.
Mayapán — the League of city-states, something like the
Achaean League of Greece — existed between the ninth and
thirteenth centuries within what is now called the Maya 'New
Empire.' Coming under the influence of the invading Toltecs
of interior Mexico, Maya architecture underwent a natural
evolution: motifs became stylized and new plastic elements
were introduced. Uxmal was one of the greatest cities of this
League. The illustrations show the House of the Magician and
the great Nunnery Quadrangle. The view was taken from the
upper terrace of the House of the Governor, looking north.

Lithographed by John C. Bourne.

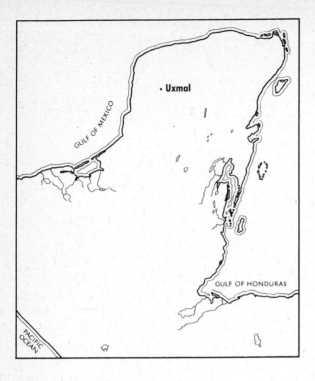

Plate IX Detail of the *Ornament over the Doorway, Casa del Gobernador, Uxmal (Yucatán)*. This structure is one of the most extensive and the best preserved in Yucatán. It has a central section and two wings separated by two transverse arches. Eleven doorways pierce the façade, whose beams were once made of *sapote* wood. The Governor's House measures 320 ft. in length, 40 ft. in depth, about 26 ft. in height. The walls are faced with masterfully cut limestone made into an elaborate stone mosaic, into which the decoration over the doorway shown here fits with perfect rhythm. This ornament — the only one perfectly preserved — is found above the seventh doorway. Its date of erection is about the eleventh century.

Lithographed by William Parrott.

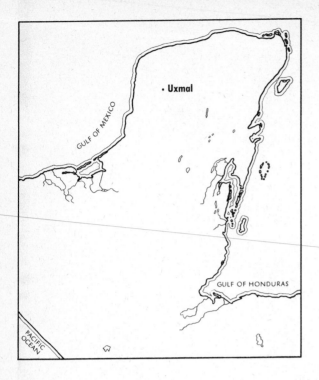

Plate X *Archway, Casa del Gobernador, Uxmal (Yucatán)*.
Sixty feet from either end of the long-fronted House of the
Governor are two transverse arches, one of which is shown in
this drawing, 20 ft. high and 25 ft. deep. They were walled
up during the occupation of Uxmal by the Maya. One of the
most strikingly beautiful stone mosaics within the Maya area,
this archway is also the best preserved. A common motif is the
stone masks of the cornices, with the elongated snout of the
Rain-God. The arabesque-like façade on the wall of the archway was used by Catherwood for the ornamental title page of
his portfolio. The original drawing of this lithograph is in the
Brooklyn Museum.

Lithographed by Andrew Picken.

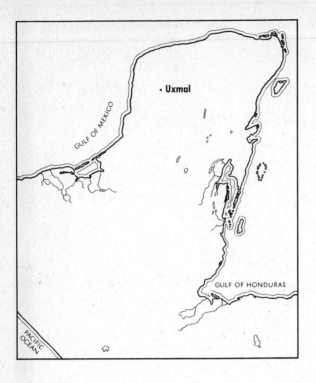

Plate XI *Gateway of the Great Teocallis, Uxmal*. The great doorway to the House of the Magician. Set upon a truncated pyramid 80 ft. high, the temple at its summit looks down upon the Nunnery Quadrangle. One of the most startling of Maya architectural concepts is the doorway, actually a gigantic mask measuring roughly 12 ft. square. Its open mouth is the entrance. The amazing feature of the mask-doorway is the fact that within the large mask are fourteen long-snouted masks of the god Itzamna. Known variously as the House of the Dwarf, Magician, Soothsayer, or, in Spanish, Adivino, the temple is reached by 240 stone steps that lead up on both sides to the top of the pyramid. The central room, curiously enough, does not face the stair but is reached from the opposite side. It was constructed at the height of the power of the League of Mayapán, about the eleventh century. The original sepia is in the United States National Museum, Washington, D. C.

Lithographed by Thomas Shotter Boys.

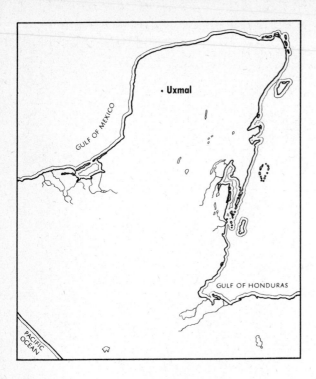

Plate XII *Ornament over the Gateway of the Great Teocallis, Uxmal*. This is the summit of the façade of the second section of the House of the Magician. It attracted. Frederick Catherwood because of the unusual stone-mosaic pattern. Eight statues, once attached to the façade, had been removed before Stephens and Catherwood arrived in 1840. The Temple was visited in 1588 by Fray Antonio de Ciudad Real, who wrote of the 'very renowned edifices of Uxmal.'

Lithographed by William Parrott.

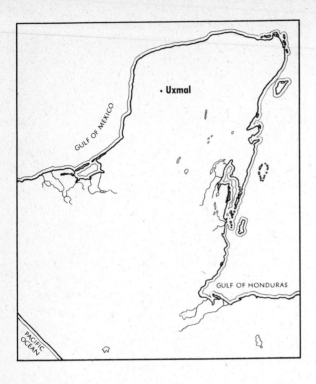

Plate XIII *General View of Uxmal . . . (Yucatán).* The second panorama of Uxmal (Plate VIII was the first), taken from
the archway of the Nunnery, looking south, is intended to
complete the general view of the great Uxmal site that covers a
square mile of Yucatán earth. Between the two mounds in the
foreground, the amorphous walls of a ruined Maya ball-court,
is the gigantic earth podium that supports a small temple called
the 'House of the Turtles' (because of a realistic stone frieze of
turtles), and to the left the rectangular-shaped House of the
Governor. The gabled structure to the right was called, fanci-
fully, 'House of the Doves,' because the perforations suggest
dovecotes. This roof comb probably held an elaborate stucco
frieze. Beyond these, in the haze of background, are other
pyramids, unnamed, with the ruins of temples atop the truncated structure.

Lithographed by Andrew Picken.

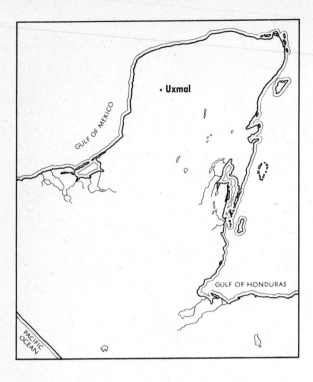

Plate XIV *Portion of a Building: Las Monjas, Uxmal.* This is the detail of the Inner Court of the Nunnery. The Nunnery — called thus by the Spanish in allusion to the ninety cell-like chambers of the architectural complex — is one of the most magnificent structures in all Mayadom. It rests on an earth podium some 15 ft. high and is composed of four buildings, all different in their ornamentation. On the west wall, of which this illustration is a detail, great carved serpents — once painted vivid green — wind in and out of a geometric pattern. This section of Uxmal now stands as it was pictured by Catherwood over a century ago. The Nunnery is now being restored by the archaeologists of the Republic of Mexico.

Lithographed by Andrew Picken.

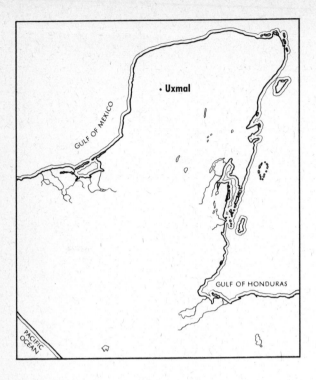

Plate XV *Portion of La Casa de Las Monjas, Uxmal.* This is
the detail of the south façade of the Nunnery. The Nunnery —
actually four great rectangular structures, low-built, heavy,
and formal — covers an area approximately 300 ft. square. The
monotonous façade of the western outer wall is broken by the
snouted masks of the long-nosed god Itzamna, the Maya god
of learning. It is, however, in the inner court that the decoration runs riot, with boldly drawn mosaic frets animated by
mytho-esthetic motifs. Catherwood's plate of the detail of the
façade of the inner court, western side, is one of the most exquisite drawings of his portfolio. The original, of which this is
only a detail, is in the Museum of the American Indian, New
York.

Lithographed by Andrew Picken.

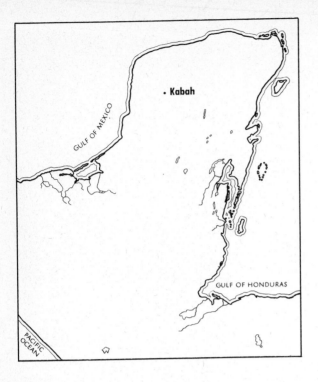

Plate XVI *General View of Kabah (Yucatán)*. Kabah, one of the constellations of the League of Mayapán, flourished at the same time as Labná, a neighboring site. The panorama of Kabah shows the three principal structures, one of which, Palacio No. I, is famous for its design of six tiers of masks that ornament the façade. In the foreground there is a solitary arch, its use unknown. From these ruins Stephens took the *sapote* beams carved with glyphs, which were burned in the fire that destroyed Catherwood's rotunda. The picture illustrates John Lloyd Stephens, in blue cutaway jacket, directing the removal of the stone-door jambs from Kabah structures, which now, after many vicissitudes, are in the Central American Hall of the American Museum of Natural History.

Lithographed by Andrew Picken.

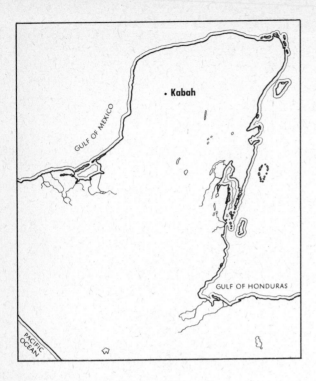

Plate XVII *Interior of Principal Building at Kabah (Yucatán).* This plate shows the manner in which the Maya used the corbeled arch. Many of the structures of archaic civilizations — the early Egyptian (at Gizeh), the walls of Tiryns at Arpino (Italy), and early Grecian structures — show a similar corbeling method. The stones were cut to special shape and laid layer upon layer until they met. The roof was heavily weighted to hold the arch, and the deep entablature created by this technique gave the Maya wide surfaces on which to exhibit excellent surface decoration.

Lithographed by Andrew Picken.

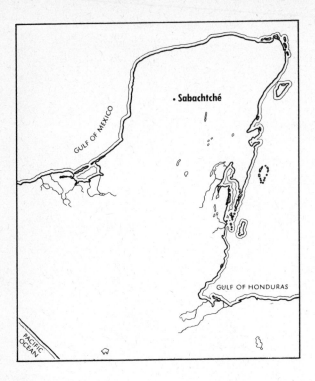

Plate XVIII *Well and Building at Sabachtsché (Yucatán).*
These ruins lie well within the orbit of the League of Mayapán. The structure here pictured, more as background to the
Indians than a detailed archaeological study, is 20 ft. long, 10 ft.
wide, built with characteristic roof-comb. This picture of the
Indian women drawing water from the *cenote* is actually a
synthesis of two scenes, since the *cenote* is located in the village
some distance from the ruins.

Lithographed by Henry Warren.

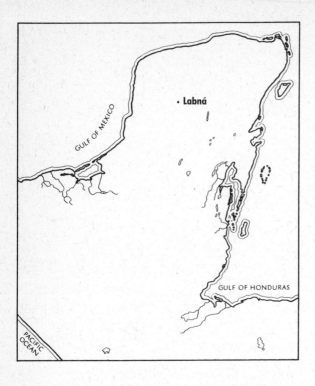

Plate XIX *Gateway at Labná (Yucatán)*. Labná, a city-state
within the political-culture orbit of the League of Mayapán, is
situated midway between Uxmal and Chichén Itzá. Its Great
Palace — architecturally similar to Sayil, with its motifs of
masks and columnettes — is one of the largest buildings in
Yucatán. Erected on a podium of rubble base, faced with cut
stone, the Great Palace is 400 ft. long and 250 ft. in depth.
Close to the palace is the famous Labná Gateway. The gateway
is a portal arch; its functions are unknown. The recesses of the
gateway are richly ornamented in stucco. Once frescoed with
color — traces of which are still visible — it was intended to
represent the sun's face surrounded by pulsating sun rays.
'The cement used in its construction,' wrote Catherwood,
'was very good — equal . . . to that found in many ancient
Roman buildings.'

Lithographed by John C. Bourne.

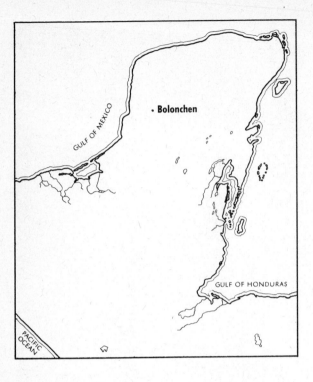

Plate **XX** *Well at Bolonchen (Yucatán).* Southward along
the Campeche trail, beyond the constellation of the city-states
that formed the Mayapán League, are Maya ruins scattered in
the dry jungle. One of these is Bolonchen, the 'Village of the
Nine Wells.' There are no rivers in Yucatán; water flows be-
neath the limestone shelf and is raised from the open-mouthed
cenotes. These *cenotes*, of immemorable age, are the basis of
our deductions about Maya culture. The well of Bolonchen
was used by the village in the dry season. There is a descent
of 200 feet to the first water. The principal ladder, illustrated
by Catherwood, is 80 feet long. The *cenote* cavern is now no
longer used; the ladder has been destroyed. The original drawing of the study of Bolonchen is in the collection of Henry
Schnackenberg, Esq., Newton, Conn.

Lithographed by Henry Warren.

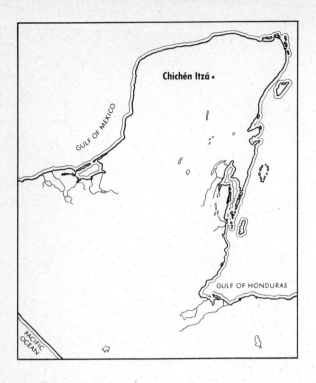

Chichén Itzá •

GULF OF MEXICO

GULF OF HONDURAS

PACIFIC OCEAN

Plate XXI *Las Monjas, Chichén Itzá (Yucatán)*. Chichén Itzá ('The Mouth of the Wells of Itzá') is the best known of Maya sites. The number of its buildings, the great Ball Court, Temple of the Warriors, its Temple of Kulkulkan, portray its importance to the Maya world. It was, in its heyday, a sacred city to which all Indians, at one time in their lives, made a pilgrimage. Occupied early in Maya history, it was abandoned and then reoccupied during the tenth and thirteenth centuries. The Red House, The House of the Three Lintels, and the Nunnery belong to the Old Empire period. The Nunnery is the oldest building at Chichén Itzá, a massive compact structure of which this illustration is only the east-end annex of the main temple. It is an L-shaped building, 35 feet wide (Catherwood fails to show its connection with the main structure) and, as seen, is elaborately decorated. The dominant decorative motif — the masks — is that of the familiar Itzamna, the protean god of rain, writing, and learning. The original of this drawing — a sepia — is in the Brooklyn Museum.

Lithographed by George Belton Moore.

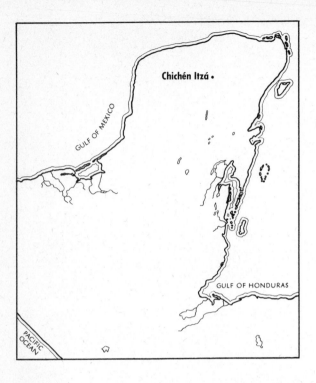

Plate XXII *Teocallis, at Chichén Itzá*. The temple of Kulkulkan, Chichén Itzá, Yucatán, the Temple of the Plumed Serpent, stands more or less in the center of Chichén Itzá. In front
— south of it — is the Sacred Well; to the north, the Ball Court;
to the east, the Temple of the Warriors. The Temple of Kulkulkan, 80 feet high, with a temple at its summit, is reached by
broad stone steps from the four sides — symbols of the four
principal directions. At the base of the northern side are two
gigantic heads of open-mouthed serpents, one of which Catherwood has drawn for effect in this, the first illustration ever
made of Chichén Itzá. The Temple of Kulkulkan is wholly
symbolic; there are two sets of stone terraces that indicate the
18-month Maya calendar; the four flights of 90 stone steps
multiply into 360 days; the last five days of the calendar year,
the *Uayeb*, were the 'five empty days' and not counted. The
Temple of Kulkulkan is now fully restored.

Lithographed by Andrew Picken.

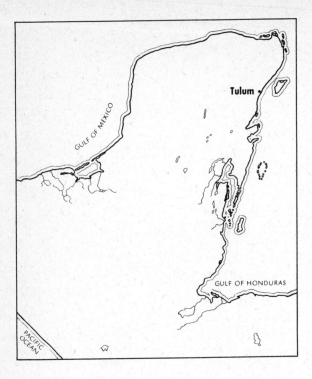

GULF OF MEXICO

Tulum

GULF OF HONDURAS

PACIFIC OCEAN

Plate XXIII *Castle, at Tuloom*. The ruins of Tulum, Quintana Roo, Mexico, a walled city, lie at the edge of the wave-washed coast of eastern Yucatán, in the department of Quintana Roo. It was the first city seen by the *conquistadores* before the conquest of Mexico. Tulum was built *c*. A. D. 560, reoccupied in the thirteenth and fourteenth centuries, and was, in all probability, functioning at the time of the conquest. The Castillo, here illustrated, is 100 feet across the base, including its two wings, and is reached by a flight of stairs. The Temple room is low-ceilinged, flat, and capped with square abaci.

Lithographed by Andrew Picken.

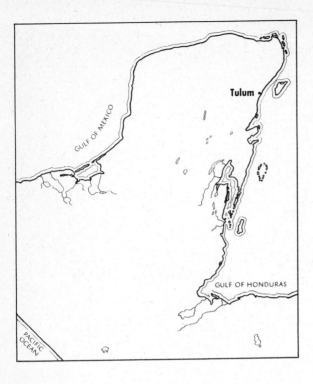

Plate XXIV *Temple, at Tuloom.* The temple of the Frescoes, Tulum, Quintana Roo, Mexico, with its figure of the Diving God on the façade, was discovered by accident. Although it lay only 250 feet from the principal temple, the trees were so thick in 1842 that it was unseen by the Stephens expedition. Dr. Cabot, hunting for wild turkeys (he may be seen in the shadows left of the temple), discovered it. Resting on a 6-foot stone terrace, the building measures 45 feet long and 26 feet deep. The interior is divided into two parallel apartments. The ceiling was wooden-beamed. An autobiographical note has been added: John L. Stephens, pictured in a blue cutaway jacket and straw hat, carries the end of a measuring line; Catherwood, in long frock coat, tight jodhpur-like white pants, holds the other end of the measuring tape. This is the only known portrait of Frederick Catherwood.

Lithographed by William Parrott.

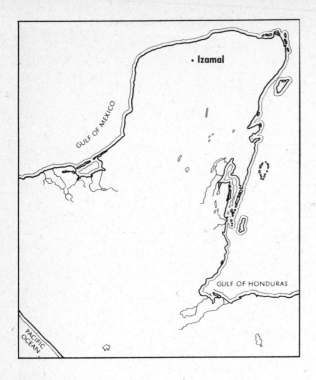

Plate XXV *Colossal Head, at Izamal (Yucatán)*. Izamal, including this colossal sculptured head, is now completely destroyed. It was the site chosen for the first Franciscan monastery in Yucatán, near Merida. The Maya structures were torn down to build the monastery, which later was directed by the contradictory, famous and infamous, Fray Diego de Landa. This stone head, drawn by Frederick Catherwood, survived the destruction of Izamal until the nineteenth century. Even as late as this, Indians burned copal incense on the small stone platform in front of the god's image. Dr. Samuel Cabot hunts a jaguar at its base — an incident that occurred during the expedition but not, however, at Izamal.

Lithographed by Henry Warren.

1. *Frederick Catherwood, Self-Portrait before Ruins of Tulum, Quintana Roo, Mexico.* This is the only known portrait of Catherwood. From *Views of Ancient Monuments,* 1844, Plate XXIV.

2. *View of Mt. Etna from Tauramina (Sicily)*. Watercolor by Frederick Catherwood,
1823. Reproduced by the courtesy of Mrs. Frederick Hoppin, New York.

3. *El 'Aqsa, the Mosque of Omar, Jerusalem.* From a drawing by Catherwood engraved
by Finden.

4. *An Interior of the Golden Gate, Jerusalem*. From a drawing by F. Catherwood engraved by E. Finden.

5. *Ruins of Djerash, Transjordania*. From a drawing by F. Catherwood attributed to Harding. Engraved by E. Finden.

6. *Colossi of Memnon — Statue of Amen-Hotep III — Thebes*. Original pencil drawing by
F. Catherwood. Reproduced by the courtesy of The British Museum.

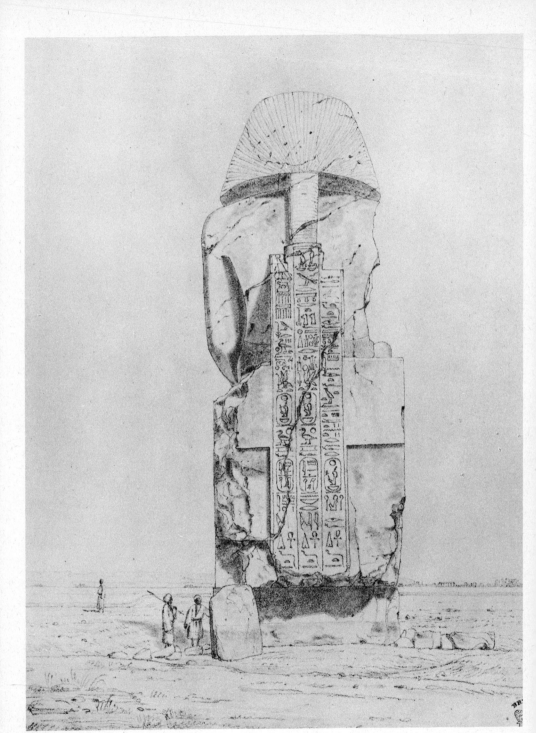

7. *Colossi of Memnon — (rear view).* Original pencil drawing by F. Catherwood. Reproduced by the courtesy of The British Museum.

8. *Yum Kax, Lord of Harvest (Maya)*. Original sepia drawing by F. Catherwood. Reproduced by the courtesy of Henry Schnackenberg.

9. *Fallen Maya Stele (D) at Copan*. Original sepia drawing by F. Catherwood. Reproduced by the courtesy of Henry Schnackenberg.

10. *Maya Stele (D)*. Lithographed from the original drawing by Frederick Catherwood that appeared in *Views of Ancient Monuments*, 1844.

II. *The Altar of the Temple of the Sun. The original drawing, engraved by Dick, appeared in Stephens's Incidents of Travel in Central America . . . 1841.*

12. *The House of the Magician, Uxmal, Yucatán.* Original sepia drawing by Frederick Catherwood. Reproduced by the courtesy of U.S. National Museum.

13. *The Nunnery, Uxmal, Yucatán.* Original sepia drawing by F. Catherwood. Reproduced by the courtesy of the Museum of the American Indian, New York.

14. *Detail of the Ruins of Sabachtsché, Yucatán*. Original watercolor by F. Catherwood.
Reproduced by the courtesy of Henry Schnackenberg.

15. *Design for a Memorial to Washington*, 1845. Lithographed by G. Thomas after a drawing by F. Catherwood. Reproduced by the courtesy of The New-York Historical Society.

16. *View of New York from Governors Island*, 1844. Engraved by Henry Paprill from a drawing by F. Catherwood. Reproduced by the courtesy of The New-York Historical Society.

CHAPTER ONE

1. *Archaeologia*, vol. II, London, 1773, p. 36.
2. The British Museum Catalogue of Printed Books, Ann Arbor, 1946.
3. *The History and Survey of London*, 4 vols., with atlas by B. Lamert, London, 1806, vol. IV, p. 75.
4. Besant, Sir Walter, *London, North of the Thames*, London, 1911, p. 588.
5. Ellis, Sir Henry, *History of Shoreditch*, London, 1846.
6. Newton, John, *Letters to a Wife*, 2 vols., London, 1793. The preface is dated, 'Charles Sq., Hoxton.'
7. Hollingshead, John, *My Life Time*, London, 1895.
8. This discovery I owe to the kindness of Mr. C. J. Jackson, Librarian of the Borough of Shoreditch, who sought out the musty records of Hoxton in order to find something of Catherwood's genealogy. His letter to me is as follows:

'Further to my letter of 11th October, 1946, I have now completed my researches into Frederick Catherwood's genealogy. The files of the local Shoreditch paper go back only as far as the end of last century, and the Assessment Books, Pavement Ledgers, Watchmen's Books, and Housemen's Report Books in our possession show no trace of the Catherwoods. With the Rate and Land Tax Books, however, I have been more fortunate. These run from 1775 to 1835, with the following results:

1775, 1788—No record of Catherwood.
1806—Nath Catherwood in residence in Charles Square (number not given),
1806—Elizabeth Catherwood in residence at 25 Charles Square.
1808—Elizabeth and Nath at No. 20.
1810—John and Nathaniel Catherwood in Charles Square (no number).
1811—ditto
1816—John Catherwood at No. 21.
1816—Elizabeth Catherwood at No. 20.
1817—ditto
1820—ditto
1821—ditto

1822—John and Nath (no number).
1835—John at No. 21.
1835—Elizabeth at No. 20.

Nathaniel, John and Elizabeth therefore resided at 20 and 21 at least until Frederick was 36. From the fact that John resided at 21 and Elizabeth at 20 I deduce that Frederick's parents were Nathaniel and Elizabeth.

I hope this information will be of assistance to you.

Yours sincerely,

C. M. Jackson,

Borough Librarian.'

Alfred Catherwood, M.D., the younger brother of Frederick, was born in Hoxton, at the same 21 Charles Square address, in 1803. He attended the University of Glasgow in 1830-31 and is shown on 'The Roll of the Graduates of the University of Glasgow from the 31st of December, 1727 to 31st December, 1897.' With short biographical notes, compiled by W. Inness Addison. On page 103 is:

'Catherwood, Alfred, C. M. 1830 M. D. 1831 London, died 19th February 1865, aged 62.'

The L. S. A. after his name in 1842 means he was late physician to the London Dispensary. He was author of *Treatise . . . on the Lungs* published in 1844 and dated from 21, Charles Sq., Hoxton. Nothing more is known of Alfred Catherwood, M. D.

9. Elmes, James, *London in the 19th Century*, London, 1830, plate 73, p. 143.
10. Birkenhead, S. B. S., *Against Oblivion: The Life of Joseph Severn*, London, New York, 1944.

CHAPTER TWO

1. Graves, Algernon, *The Royal Academy of Arts: A Complete Dictionary of Contributors and Their Work from Its Foundation in 1769 to 1904*, 'Michael Meredith,' London, 1905-6.
2. Whitley, William T., *Art in England*, 1800-1820, London, 1927.
3. Rollins, Hyder E., *The Keats Circle . . .* (1806-1878), 2 vols., Cambridge, 1948.
4. Drawings by William Brockedon. British Museum 2515. One hundred and four portraits in pencil on paper drawn between 1824 and 1849 of contemporary persons. From the collections of Colonel Noel Baxendale.
5. Plate XXIV, *Views of Ancient Monuments in Central America . . .* published by Frederick Catherwood, London, 1844. Catherwood stands to the right of the plate holding the surveyor's tape. John Lloyd Stephens,

in blue cutaway jacket, walks with the tape, and in the shadows to the left of the Tulum Temples, Dr. Samuel Cabot, shotgun in hand, stalks an ocellated turkey.

6. Birnstingl, H. J., *Sir John Soane*, London, 1925.

7. Ibid. p. 16.

8. Blomfield, Reginald, *Architectural Drawings and Draughtsmen*, London, 1912, p. 64.

9. Graves, Algernon, *The Royal Academy of Arts: A Complete Dictionary of Contributors and Their Work from Its Foundation in 1769 to 1904*, 'Catherwood,' London, 1905-6.

    1820, #973 Buckingham Gate, Adelphi. F. Catherwood, Architect, 19 Charles Sq., Hoxton.

CHAPTER THREE

1. *Severn Collections*, Correspondence in the Keats Museum, Hampstead; Joseph Severn to Maria Severn, dated Rome, 15 September 1821.

2. Ibid. Joseph Severn to Tom Severn, dated Rome, 24 March 1822.

3. *Dictionary of National Biography; Royal Institute of British Architects Transactions Report* 1836, London, 1836; Memoir in *Gentleman's Magazine, New Series*, London, 1836, vol. IV, pp. 325, 670.

4. *The Dictionary of Architecture*, vol. II, 'Catherwood' by J. J. Scoles, London, 18(52)53-92.

5. Fox, Henry Edward, *The Journal of Henry Fox*, London, 1923, p. 248.

6. Birkenhead, S. B. S., op. cit., p. 151.

7. Fox, H. E., op. cit., p. 229.

8. *Severn Collections*, op. cit. Joseph Severn to Maria Severn, dated Rome, 21 December 1821.

9. *Severn Collections*, op. cit. Joseph Severn to Tom Severn, dated Rome, 24 March 1822.

10. *The Dictionary of Architecture*, 'Catacombs,' illustrated by Frederick Catherwood, Henry Parke, and J. J. Scoles from sketches made in 1823.

11. Stephens, John Lloyd, *Incidents of Travel in Central America, Chiapas, and Yucatán*, 2 vols, New York, 1841.

12. Haslip, Joan, *Lady Hester Stanhope*, Penguin edition, London, 1934.

13. Hay, Robert, British Museum Add. MS. 31054, ff. 41, 42, 87.

14. *Severn Collections*, op. cit. Joseph Severn to Maria Severn, dated Rome, 12 December 1825.

15. *The Dictionary of Architecture*, vol. II, 'Catherwood.'

16. Graves, Algernon, op. cit.: 1828—559 Sketch of Temple in Nubia; 615 Pyramid; 1087 Temple.

17. Hay, Robert, *Manuscript Collections in the British Museum,* 49 vols., Add. MS. 29, 812-29, -860.

Among the drawings in the Hay and Burton MSS. in the British Museum done by Catherwood are:

Original sketch and measurements of Gizeh Pyr. etc. Add. MS. 29,812, ff. 34, 39, 41-56.

Letter from Catherwood respecting Pyramid drawings, Add. MS. 29,859, f. 39.

Section of the Step Pyramid Sakkara, Add. MS. 29,812, f. 83.

Plan of brick ruins at Et Till, Add. MS. 29,814, f. 20.

Plan of Araba, Add. MS. 29,814, f. 110, May 1833.

Plan of Dendera, Add. MS. 29,814, f. 119, 1833.

Plan of Kurneh forming part of a grand plan of Thebes (1832 or 33). On this map of Thebes see *Annales du Service,* VII, p. 78, and an unfinished plan of Thebes among the Burton MSS. in the British Museum Add. MS. 25,658, f. 1.

Also a letter from Catherwood to Robert Hay, Add. MS. 29,816.

Dear Sir,

I am sorry that I cannot leave the drawings of the Pyramids in a more perfect state. The only level I had unfortunately fell and broke before I had measured little more than half way up the Pyramid. As it could not be replaced at Cairo I was obliged to wait the arrival of Mr. Arundale to recommence operations and this joined to a violent attack of Opthamalia will explain the reason of the five drawings not being made. I however will finish them on my return to England before publication without further remuneration and I only repeat that circumstances prevents my leaving them in a perfect state.

With kind regards to Mrs. Hay believe me Dear Sir.

Yours very truly,

F. Catherwood

18. Ibid. MS. 29,816.

19. Ibid. MS. 29,827.

20. James Haliburton left to the British Museum 67 volumes (Add. MSS. 25,613-75) of diaries, notes, drawings. There is, doubtlessly, if one has the patience to leaf through the volumes, considerable personal material on Catherwood.

21. Hay, Robert, op. cit. MS. 29,813.

22. Ibid. MS. 29,834.

23. Ibid. MS. 29,812-29, 845. Catherwood also accompanied George Alexander Hoskins, on 14 October 1832, to the Oasis of Kharga (80 miles east of Thebes). Hoskins, who has left a narrative of the expedition, *A Visit to the Great Oasis of the Libyan Desert,* London, 1837, spoke

148

often of Catherwood, whom he called 'Mr. C.'; 'A pistol with seven barrels, belonging to Mr. C. was considered by the Arabs who saw it, as a most formidable weapon and the fame of it was widely spread in the valley of the Nile' (p. 26). Yet, despite the fact that Catherwood is mentioned in some detail, there is no physical description of him.

24. *The Dictionary of Architecture*, op. cit., 'Catherwood.'

25. Ibid. 'Tomb of Dugga.'

26. Catherwood, Frederick, 'Account of the Punico-Libyan Monument at Dugga and the Remains of an Ancient Structure at Bless, near the site of Ancient Carthage,' *Transactions of the American Ethnological Society*, New York, 1845, vol. i, pp. 477-91; 7 figures in text.

   The founder of the Royal Institute of British Architects, T. J. Donaldson, writing of the tomb, said: 'My lamented and valued friend Frederick Catherwood author of the beautiful work on the monuments of Central America traveled in Africa and took a camera lucida view of this tomb . . . in 1832.'

27. Fergusson, James, *History of Architecture*, 2 vols., New York, 1874, vol. i, pp. 359-68. Fig. 242 by Catherwood. Donaldson, T. J., 'Recent Travels in Algiers and Tunis,' *R.I.B.A. Sessional Papers*, 1876-7, pp. 33-47. Plate by Catherwood. Gesenius, Guil, *Scriptures Linguaeque Phoeniciae*, Caput sextum Punico Numidicae. Plates by Catherwood, Lipsiae, 1837.

28. Arundale, F., *Illustrations of Jerusalem and Mt. Sinai, Including the Most Interesting Sites between Grand Cairo and Beyrout*, London, 1837. Francis Arundale was drawn by William Brockedon in September 1829. The pencil sketch is now in the British National Portrait Gallery (2515:36).

29. *Description of a View of the Ruins of the Temple of Baalbec*, drawn by Robert Burford from sketches by F. Catherwood, London, 1844.

30. Taken from a letter written to W. H. Bartlett and printed in *Walks about the City and Environs of Jerusalem* by W. H. Bartlett, London, 1842, under title of 'Mr. Catherwood's Adventure' (pp. 148-65).

31. *Plan of Jerusalem*, by F. Catherwood, Architect, July 1835, London. Published 1 Aug 1835 by F. Catherwood, 21 Charles Square, Hoxton. 'The Mosque of Omar,' drawn by David Roberts from a sketch by F. Catherwood, plate 75, Horne's *Landscape Illustrations of the Bible*, 1836. 'Jerusalem,' Pulpit on the platform of the Mosque of Omar, drawn by Samuel Prout from a sketch by F. Catherwood, plate 72. 'A View of the Interior of the Mosque of Omar,' a watercolor exhibited at the National Academy of Design in 1843, 285.

32. 27 November, 'commenced assisting Mr. Catherwood making measure-ments of the plan [of the court surrounding the Mosque].' 11 December, 'made a general view of the interior of the Mosque.' 12 December, 'Began a section of the great Mosque. Mr. Catherwood and myself took some heights with the sextant.' From Francis Arundale's *Illustrations of Jerusalem and Mount Sinai Including the Most Interesting Sites between Grand Cairo and Beyrout*, London, 1837.

33. 'After Catherwood's death in 1850 [actually 1854] his papers came into my hands . . .' wrote James Fergusson in 1878. These papers, which included the great portfolio of drawings of the 'Mosque of Omar' have also disappeared.

34. Fergusson, James, *An Essay on the Ancient Topography of Jerusalem*, London, 1847. Two of Catherwood's plates are reproduced.

In addition to the above, Catherwood's material was used in the follow-ing publications:

Finden, William, *Landscape Illustrations of the Bible*, 2 vols., London, 1836. Eleven plates attributed to Frederick Catherwood.

Bartlett, W. H., *Walks about the City and Environs of Jerusalem*, London, 1842; *Jerusalem Revisited*, London, 1854.

Robinson, Edward, *Palestine*, 2 vols., New York, 1847.

Fergusson, James, *The Temple of the Jews*, London, 1878; *The Holy Sepulchre*, London, 1865; *Essay on the Ancient Topography of Jerusalem*, London, 1844.

Smith, H. C., *Dictionary of the Bible*, London, 1852.

Williams, George, *The Holy City*, 2 vols., London, 1844.

With the exception of these fragmentary scorings, all of the drawings of Frederick Catherwood's Palestinian researches seem to have disappeared. However, only comparatively recently Mr. Laurence Gomme of Bren-tano's Rare Book Department, New York, sold ten 8" x 10" pencil draw-ings by Catherwood on the Holy Land. They are signed 'F. C.' and 'F. Catherwood.' Their present whereabouts are unknown.

CHAPTER FOUR

1. Chancellor, E. Beresford, *The Pleasure Haunts of London*, London 1925, pp. 271-97.

2. Born, Wolfgang, *American Landscape Painting*, New Haven, 1948.

Literature on the History of Panoramas

Panorama und diorama. In Repartorium der technischen literatur die jahre 1823 bis einschl. 1853 umfassend. Zum gebrauche der Koniglich technischer deputation für gewerbe bearbeitet von Dr. Schubarth, p. 648, Berlin, 1856.

Bapst, Germain, *Essai sur l'histoire des panoramas et des dioramas* . . . avec illustrations inédites de M. Edouard Detaille, Paris, 1891.

Arrowsmith, 'Diorama,' *London Journal of Arts and Sciences*, London, 1st ser., vol. 9, p. 337.

'Panorama,' *Repertory of Arts, Manufacture and Agriculture*, London, 2nd ser., vol. 46, p. 257.

'Panorama,' *Aingler's polytichcisches journal*, vol. 17, p. 316.

Ackermann, 'Pockilorama,' *The Repository of Arts, Literature, Fashions*, London, 3rd ser., vol. 7, p. 176.

'Diorama,' *The Mechanic's Magazine*, London, vol. 5, p. 314; vol. 6, pp. 289, 318.

'Georama,' *Recueil industriel*, Paris, vol. 2, p. 219. Description des machines et procédés consignés dans les brevets d'invention.

Prevost, 'Panoramen zu malen,' *Brevets d'invention, Meth.*, Paris, vol. 13, no. 5.

'Panoramas,' *Recueil industriel*, Paris, vol. 7, p. 191.

Barbaron, 'Panorama voyageur,' *Brevets d'invention*, Paris, vol. 7, p. 191.

Nepveu, 'Panorama portatif,' *Brevets d'invention*, Paris, vol. 29, p. 215.

'On the Construction of Panoramas,' *Journal des connaissances usuelles et pratiques*, Paris, vol. 25, p. 87.

'Daguerre's Dioramen,' Recueil de la societé polytechnique, Paris, 3rd ser., vol. 9, p. 52.

'Diorama,' *Edinburgh New Philosophical Journal*, Edinburgh, vol. 32, p. 142; vol. 34, p. 275; vol. 35, p. 53.

Vallet and Morgan, 'Diorama de salon,' *Brevets d'invention*, Paris, vol. 51, p. 381.

3. Hollingshead, John, *The Story of Leicester Square*, London, 1892; Cunningham, George H., *London*, New York, 1947; Clunn, Harold P., *The Face of London*, London, 1932; Kent, William, *An Encyclopedia of London*, London, 1937.

4. Mitchell, Robert, *Barker's Panorama*, London, 1801.

5. Dobson, Austin, *At Prior Park*, in which is detailed the 'Eidophusikon,' London, 1892.

6. Burford, Robert, *Description of the View of the City of New York*, painted by Robert Burford, London, 1834; *Description of a View of the City of Jerusalem* . . . Now exhibiting at The Panorama, Leicester Square . . . *From Drawings taken in 1834 by Mr. F. Catherwood, Architect*, London, 1835; *Description of a View of the Great Temple of Karnak and the Surrounding City of Thebes* . . . Now exhibiting at The Panorama, Leicester Square . . . *From Drawings, taken by Mr. F. Catherwood, Architect*, London, 1839; *Description of a View of the Ruins of the Temple of Baalbec* . . . Painted by the Proprietor Robert Burford . . . *From Drawings taken on the spot by F. Catherwood, Esq.*, London, 1844.

CHAPTER FIVE

1. Newton, Roger Hale, *Town & Davis, Architects*, New York, 1942.
2. This material on Frederick Diaper was taken from the obituaries in the *New-York Herald*, 13 September 1906, and *New York Tribune*, 13 September 1906, and Austin B. Keep, *History of the New York Society Library*.

Institute of British Architects
3. To Frederick Catherwood esq., Hony & Corresponding Member

43, King Street, Covent Garden
28, April 1836

Dear Catherwood,

It is with my pleasure that I communicate to you thus officially your election as Honorary & Corresponding Member of our Body. Although the members who have so long known you much regret your contemplated departure, yet they avail themselves of this very circumstance to create a connecting link between you and us which may induce you to fulfil the claims which we shall have upon you by occasionally sending us information from the other side of the Atlantic. You are doubtless aware that our Laws preclude our electing an English architect a Member of our Body while he resides in England other than as an associate or Fellow. We shall therefore hope that when you come to fix your wandering steps in this country you will become one of the Body in that class *to which you are so entitled.*

May success attend you is the wish not only of every one of yr. Brother Members of the Institute but especially of your old Fellow Student.

Thos L. Donaldson
Hony Secy.

PS By A special Resolution passed on Monday Evening, when you presented that famous drawing of the section of *Raphaels Loggie of the Vatican* to the Institute I am directed to convey to you the cordial thanks of the Members for this valuable mark of your regard. When we look at it we shall think of our absent Brother and hope that you may at such moments be thinking of us, & collecting memoranda to communicate to the Institute [New-York Historical Society].

4. John R. Bartlett Correspondence, John Carter Brown Library, Providence, R. I.

466 Houston Street, N. Y.
November 25, 1838.

J. Bartlett esq.,
Dear Sir,

I am sorry I did not see you yesterday as in case you have not met with any lodgings to your mind I had a proposition to make respecting the house I am now in. As I shall probably take my little boy with me to England Mrs. C. does not feel inclined to live in a House by herself and I thought if you could not do any better you might occupy the House reserving one parlour and bedroom for Mrs. C. and her baby . . .

F. Catherwood

5. Means, Philip Ainsworth, *Newport Tower*, New York, 1942, pp. 1, 52, 54, 56, 58, 81, 89, 93, 98, 140-42.

6. Rafn, Carl Christian, 'Account of an Ancient Structure in Newport, Rhode Island,' *Memoires de la Societe des Antiquaries du Nord*, Copenhagen, 1839, pp. 361-85. Contains illustrations by Catherwood.

7. Catherwood, Frederick, *Account Book, Panorama, New York*, MS. Journal in the collections of the New-York Historical Society.

8. *New York Mirror*, 18 August 1838.

9. Mason, J. Alden, 'A Mississippi Panorama,' *Bulletin for the Society for Pennsylvania Archaeology*, vol. 12, January 1942, pp. 14-16.

10. Catherwood, F., *Account Book*, op. cit. p. 4.

11. *New York Mirror*, 29 June 1839.

12. Lancour, Harold, *American Art Auction Catalogues* (1785-1942), New York Public Library, New York, 1944, p. 26, 17 April 1839. Auctioned off by Aaron Levy, 151 Broadway, 25 April 1839.

13. Cowdrey, Bartlett, 'W. H. Bartlett and the American Scene,' *New York Historical Journal*, New-York State Hist. Association, vol. XXVI no. 4 388-400 October 1941.

CHAPTER SIX

1. The first books published on the Maya Civilization were:

Del Rio, Antonio, and Cabrera, P. F., *Description of the Ruins of an Ancient City, Discovered Near Palenque*, with illustrations by Jean Frederic de Waldeck, London, 1822.

Castañeda, Lenoir, Warden, Fracy, and St. Priest, *Relation des trois expêditions du Capitain Dupaix, 1805-07, pour la recherche des antiquités du pays, notamment celles de Mitla et de Palenque etc.*, 2 vols., Paris, 1834.

Kingsborough, Edward King, *Antiquities of Mexico*, 9 vols., London, 1831-48.

Galindo, Juan, 'The Ruins of Copán in Central America,' *Proceedings of the American Antiquarian Society*, 1835, vol. II, pp. 543-50.

2. Hagen, Victor Wolfgang von, 'Waldeck, Fantastic Archaeologist,' *Natural History Magazine*, December, 1946, vol. 55, no. 10; *Maya Ex-*

plorer, University of Oklahoma Press, 1947. 'Waldeck,' pp. 72, 152-5, 169, 188, 193, 196, 222; and Cline, Howard F., 'The Apochryphal Early Career of J. F. de Waldeck, Pioneer Americanist,' *Acta Americana,* Mexico, 1947, vol. v, no. 4, pp. 278-300.

3. Bartlett, John Russell, MS. Journal in the John Carter Brown Library, pp. 37-40.

4. Published in *Transactions of the American Antiquarian Society,* vol. II, pp. 543-50.

5. Diego Garcia de Palacio, an official of the Audiencia de Guatemala, who visited the ruins of Copán in 1576—not many years after the conquest—wrote a letter to his liege Philip II about Copán. He thought the monolithic sculptures were of Europeans, 'for the first are dressed in military garments wholly Spanish as though the demon could have shown the Spaniard thus arrayed to the Indians even before the coming of them to these shores.' And the befuddled official thought he saw 'claps and girdles and the sword belts of the cavaliers . . . short breeches, frilled collar, breastplate . . . bracelets . . . helmets. . .' But it was not to Palacio's letter,' writes Dr. Maudslay, 'which was only comparatively recently unearthed from the Spanish archives, but to the charming pages of Stephens and the beautiful drawings of Catherwood that the world in general is indebted for a knowledge of the wonder of Copán.' Maudslay, Alfred P., 'Biologia Centrali-Americana,' in *Archaeology,* London, 1889-1902.

6. Stephens, John L., *Incidents of Travel in Central America . . .* 2 vols., New York, 1841, vol. I, pp. 117-25.

7. Kelemen, Pál, *Medieval American Art,* 2 vols., I, Text, II, Plates, New York, 1943. pp. 1-8.

8. Morley, S. G., *The Ancient Maya,* University of Stanford Press, Palo Alto, 1946. 'The rise and spread of the Maya Civilization-Old Empire,' ch. IV, pp. 54-67.

9. Morley, S. G., *The Inscriptions at Copán,* Washington, 1920, pp. 226, 322. The identification of Catherwood's drawings are Plate 4 (Stele C); Plate 5 (Stele D); Plate 3 (Stele F); Plate I (Stele H).

10. Maudslay, Alfred P., 'Biologia Centrali-Americana,' *Archaeology,* London, 1889-1902. Text, p. 3, 'Stephens and Catherwood were the pioneers in this work and their very accurate and beautifully illustrated works will always remain of the greatest value to the student of American archaeology.' Joyce, T. A., *British Museum Guide to the Maudslay Collection of Maya Sculptures,* p. 5; 'The permanent value of Stephens' account lies not only in the accuracy of his descriptions, but in the

illustrations which accompany his text. These were the work of an English artist, Frederick Catherwood, and the correctness of his drawings remarkable for the time when Maya hieroglyphics were an unknown thing, provides the chief reason why Stephens' books may be regarded as classic.'

11. Stele E (Catherwood's figure 13); Stele F (figure 11 in Stephens', *Incidents of Travel in Central America*, vol. I, New York, 1841). Stephens proposed to buy the entire site, float some of the sculptures down the river, send them to New York, and found a Museum for American Antiquities. 'I called upon Senor Payes . . . and opened negotiations for the ruins. Senor Payes consulted with the French Consul General, who put an exaggerated value upon the ruins . . . and so the monuments remain where they were undiscovered.' Stephens, *Incidents of Travel in Central America*, vol. II, p. 124.

See also Morley, S. G., *Guide Book to the Ruins of Quiriguá*, Washington, 1935.

12. Walker and Caddy were not killed on their visit to Palenque. They remained two weeks at Palenque. There Caddy, who was a gifted artist, made several drawings. The manuscript, *City of Palenque*, 1840, consists of 36 pages of text portfolio, 15 x 21 inches, containing a plan of the palace, 24 sepia paintings, a folding map of the peninsula of Yucatán, and a sketch map of the ruins. On Captain Caddy's return to England, he had intended to publish it. He had read it before the Society of Antiquarians on 13 January 1842, but the publications of Stephens and Catherwood forestalled him. The late Marshall Saville found these originals by contacting Miss Alice Caddy, the granddaughter of the Captain, and these were placed in his hands 'for publication.' But Professor Saville died before they could be published and they rest, with most of the papers on his property, in the possession of his son, Mr. Randolph Saville of New York. Of Caddy's drawings Saville wrote: 'The port-folio contains some sketches not found in Stephens' work and a number of drawings are more accurate than those of Catherwood. While it adds but little to our knowledge of the ruins . . . yet the artistic quality of Captain Caddy's work merits its publication; indeed, it is highly important to thus record the results of all pioneer researches, as the ruins have deteriorated considerably since the early stage of the last century.' *Indian Notes and Monographs*, vol. VI, no. 5, Heye Foundation, New York, 1928. Caddy is listed in the military lists of England as follows:

John Herbert Caddy
   Gentleman-Cadet 26 March 1816
   2nd Lieutenant 29 July 1825
   1st Lt. 31 Dec 1827
   2nd Captain 13 August 1840
   Retired on half-pay 28 May 1844.

The only recorded publication of Caddy is: 'Eight coloured Aquatint *Views in the West Indies* by Lt. H. A. Caddy (St. Vincent, St. Kitts, St. Lucia, Dominica) engraved by Westall, Fielding, &c and published by Ackermann,' London, 1837.

13. Elliott-Joyce, L. E., *Central America*, New York, 1925.

14. Presumably Frederick Chatfield, Chargé d'affaires of Great Britain in Guatemala 16 June 1849, and before that British Consul General in Guatemala from 1842-7, *Foreign Office List Forming a Complete Diplomatic and Consular Handbook, compiled by Sir Edward Hertslet*, 1901.

15. Kelemen, Pál, *Medieval American Art*, New York 1943, vol. 1, p. 65.

16. Stephens, John Lloyd, *Incidents of Travel in Central America*, New York, 1841, vol. II.

17. Catherwood footnote to the London 1854 edition of Stephens' *Incidents of Travel in Central America*, p. 475.

18. Stephens, op. cit.

19. *The Correspondence of William Hickling Prescott*, 1823-1847, Boston, 1927, pp. 210, 293.

20. Fanny Calderón de la Barca, a sprightly Scotch woman, Prescott's contemporary, was Frances Erskine Inglis, a descendant of the Earls of Buchan. Her mother established a school in Boston where Fanny and her sister Kate taught for several years. She married Angel Calderón de la Barca, who was then the Spanish Minister in Washington. She helped Prescott on his *Conquest of Mexico*, and wrote the charming *Life in Mexico*, London, 1843.

21. Stephens wrote to Prescott, 24 September 1841: 'I gave Friederichsthal a *carte du pays* for Yucatán and the result is a publication in the newspapers, impeaching the correctness of Mr. Catherwood's drawings. I did not see him when he passed through this city and cannot believe that he authorized the unfounded publication.' Catherwood commented:

The Ruins of Central America. Gentlemen: In the absence of Mr. Stephens from New York, allow me to say a few words in explanation of an article in the Journal of the 24th instant. It is there stated, that on a recent visit of the Chevalier Fredericksthal, who is represented as having just returned from Central America, after exploring the ruins of that country during a period of nine months, that the magnified impressions from his Daguerreotype views were compared with sketches in the work of Messrs. Stephens and Catherwood, which sketches in every case were found 'defective, imperfect and different from the impressions.' Now this would lead the reader to suppose that the Chevalier had visited Central America on his late excursion, whereas such is not the case, he not having set foot in that country; not having seen Copán, Quinqua, Santa Cruz del Quiche, Palenque, etc., and of course having no daguerreotype view of any of them. I would ask how could any comparison be made with those published in Mr. Stephens' work? Indeed, from the local position of the greater number of the objects, the daguerreotype could not have been used at all. The fact is simply this: nine or ten months ago, the Chevalier Fredericksthal requested Mr. Stephens to point out to him a route in that region of the world which had not been visited, and Mr. S. named Yucatán as being less known than any other, and the Chevalier accordingly confined his researches to that section of the country, and the only place which we visited in common was Uxmal. At this place, owing to my illness, we remained but one or two days, and I made in all three drawings, one being a view, another a ground plan, (which I have never heard of the Daguerreotype being yet able to accomplish,) and the third a fragment of a building. It follows, that of seventy-seven drawings in Mr. Stephens' work, there are only two with which a comparison could by possibility have been made, and it is not at all likely that in so vast a field of ruins as Uxmal, the Chevalier and myself should have hit upon the same points of view, and I am therefore at a loss to understand how a comparison could have been made between objects which I trust I have shown are totally dissimilar.

Yours respectfully,
F. Catherwood.

New York, 25th August, 1841

From *The New York Journal of Commerce*.

CHAPTER SEVEN

1. Dr. Samuel Cabot (1815-85), Boston surgeon and ornithologist. His collection of Yucatán birds was the first from that area and is housed in the Museum of Comparative Zoology at Harvard. See, 'Samuel Cabot,' *Maya Explorer*, 1947, pp. 205-11.
2. Stephens, John L., *Incidents of Travel in Yucatán*, vol. 1, p. 174.
3. These Maya sculptures—now called the *Stephens' Stones*—arrived in New York City after a fire had destroyed all else of the Maya expedition. Stephens then presented them to John Cruger to be placed in a molding romantic wall on his Cruger's Island in the Hudson near Barrytown. There for a half century the Maya carvings remained until they were rediscovered by Messrs. Morley and Spinden, purchased for and brought to the American Museum of Natural History, where they are now.

1. Hone, Philip, *Diary of Philip Hone*, MSS. 20 volumes, vol. 9, p. 380, New-York Historical Society Collections.
2. *New-York Herald*, 30 July 1842, p. 2.
3. *New-York Herald*, 1 August 1842, p. 2.
4. Prud'homme, John Francis Eugene, N. A., 1800-1892; Jones, Alfred, N. A., 1819-1900; Johnson, David, N. A., 1827-1909; Rolph, John A., N. A., 1799-1862; Halbert, G., active between 1835-46.
5. Prescott, William Hickling, *Correspondence 1833-1847*, edited by Roger Wolcott, Boston, 1925, p. 341.
6. Prescott, op cit., p. 341.
7. Edward Robinson, founder of Palestinian archaeology, author of *Biblical Researches in Palestine, Mount Sinai and Arabia Petraea*, 2 vols., New York, 1841.
8. *Proceedings of the New-York Historical Society*, 2 May 1843, pp. 53-7.
9. 'Mr. Catherwood is the only artist and antiquarian who has visited and studied the most celebrated ruins of the other hemisphere and those of America. Ten years of his life were diligently employed in studying and taking correct drawings of the ancient architectural monuments of Egypt, Syria, Greece, and Northern Africa. No man was better qualified to point out, in all their details, in the explanations that would accompany the plates, both the analogies and dissimilarities between these celebrated remains and those of our own world.'
10. *Boston Semi-Weekly Advertiser*, vol. LXXX, no. 6474, 10 May 1843:

The Publication of the Drawings of Catherwood Illustrating the Ruins of the Cities Visited by Stephens. It is proposed by the Harpers, if 300 subscribers can be obtained at $100 each, to publish in full size the larger drawings which Mr. Catherwood has made of the ruins of Central America. Miniature copies of these drawings are published in Mr. Stephens' book, but this proposal goes to publishing in larger size the details of these drawings, with descriptions, so that the reader can see and perceive what in reality they are. The Harpers are not willing to undertake so great work without some prospect of remuneration, and they ask, therefore, for a subscription. The work, if undertaken, will be done, we presume in the first style, somewhat in the character of the drawings of the French *savants*, who accompanied Bonaparte in his Egyptian expedition.

The Historical Society of this city has taken up the matter with some interest. If the necessary number of subscribers are obtained, the work is to be issued under their auspices. The work will be an honor to the literature, and to the enterprise of the country, and will, no doubt, command an extensive attention in Europe. Mr. Gallatin justly remarked that in the qualifications of the artist, Mr. Catherwood, there was this peculiar recommendation that he alone of travellers who had visited the antiquities and the ruins of Africa and the Mediterranean, has also visited and drawn these ruins of the new world. The Library of the Historical Society of the University now has in it several of the original drawings of Mr. Catherwood. It is to be opened on Friday evening for such persons as wish to see them, which view, it is hoped, will induce many to subscribe.

11. *Boston Semi-Weekly Advertiser*, Saturday, vol. LXXX, no. 6481, 3 June 1843: *Antiquities of Central America*. Proposals have been issued at New York by Messrs. Bartlett & Welford, for publishing a work entitled the Monumental Antiquities of America by John L. Stephens, whose descriptions of these antiquities have been read with so much interest; with one hundred illustrations on a large scale, to be engraved and executed in the highest style which the state of the arts will admit of, and drawn by Mr. Catherwood. Fifteen specimen drawings, prepared for this work, are now exhibited at the bookstore of Messrs. Tappan and Dennet, which those who take an interest in it, and are disposed to see the style of execution, are invited to examine. The great expense of such a publication obliges the publishers to defer proceeding in it until they can secure the sale of a certain number of copies. It has met with a favorable reception in New York, and we hope that in this city it will meet with similar favor, and a patronage proportioned to its merits. The following resolutions are a sufficient attestation to the value of the work, and with the evidence afforded by the specimens of drawings above referred to, will enable the patrons of literature and the arts, to decide whether they will lend it their aid.

12. Prescott, op. cit., p. 366.
13. Ibid. pp. 381-2.
14. Ibid. p. 427.
15. *The Civil Engineer and Architects Journal*, 1 February 1844, pp. 92-4.
16. Fergusson, James, *History of Architecture in All Countries*, 2 vols., London, 1874.
17. Prescott, op. cit., p. 464.
18. Humboldt, Alexander von, *Letters to Varnhagen Von Ense*, London, 1860.

CHAPTER NINE

1. Cowdrey, Bartlett, editor, *National Academy of Design Exhibition Record* 1826-60, 'Frederick Catherwood,' 2 vols., New-York Historical Society, New York, 1942, pp. 72-3.
2. Phelps-Stokes, I. N., *The Iconography of Manhattan Island*, 1498-1909, 5 vols., New York, 1922-6, vol. III, pp. 697-8, plate 131.

3. Pine, John B., *The Story of Gramercy Park*, 1831-1931, New York, 1934, pp. 13-14.
4. Wilson, James Grant, *The Memorial History of the City of New York*, 4 vols., New York, 1893, vol. IV, pp. 209-10; and Barck, Dorothy, *Historical Society Quarterly Bulletin*, New York, 1931, vol. XV, no. 3, pp. 79-88.
5. 'In 1842,' wrote John R. Bartlett, the scholarly bookseller of the Astor House Bookshop, 'I suggested to Mr. Gallatin the idea of a new Society, the attention of which should be devoted to Geography, Archaeology, Philology and to enquiries generally connected with the human race. . . Mr. Gallatin was pleased with my suggestion, and I determined to propose the same thing to other gentlemen. All with whom I spoke, and these were the gentlemen who had devoted more (or) less time to the subjects which we proposed to devote ourselves, had written books, or essays upon these subjects or had become noted as travellers in foreign countries. These gentlemen accordingly met at my house to exchange views preparatory to an organization. Those present on this occasion were Mr. Gallatin, John L. Stevens [Stephens] the distinguished traveller, *Mr. Catherwood*, Reverend Dr. E. Robinson, Reverend Dr. F. S. Hawks, Mr. Charles Welford, Henry R. Schoolcraft (etc.). . .' The result was the formation of the American Ethnological Society.

On December 7, 1842, the American Ethnological Society, the first of its kind in America, came into being. 'The object of this Society shall comprise inquiries into the origin, progress and characteristics of the various races of Man.' Albert Gallatin was its President, Bartlett, its Secretary, and the name of Frederick Catherwood stood among the foremost scholars of America. *John R. Bartlett MS. Journal*, John Carter Brown Library, pp. 320-33.

In addition to Stephens, Gallatin, Robinson, Schoolcraft, Bartlett, Catherwood, and Charles Welford, the original members included Caleb Atwater, Daniel Drake, Dr. Samuel Morton, John Pickering, William H. Prescott, George Ticknor, John Torry, and Henry Wheaton.
6. Catherwood, Frederick, 'Account of the Punico-Libyan Monument at Dugga and the Remains of an Ancient Structure at Bless, near the Site of Ancient Carthage,' *Transactions of the American Ethnological Society*, New York, 1845, vol. I, pp. 477-91; 7 figures in text.

CHAPTER TEN

1. 'Report of the London Committee of Management of the Demerara Railway Read at the General Meeting of the Shareholders Held at the

London Tavern on 15 April 1847 . . . and the Report of Frederick Catherwood, Esq., C. E. Engineer of the said Company.'

2. Catherwood, Frederick, editor, Stephens' *Incidents of Travel in Central America* . . . London, 1854, preface, p. vi.

3. Report to the London Committee, MS., op. cit.:

Appendix A, Report of Mr. F. Catherwood, C.E., On the Construction of a Railway from Georgetown to Mahica.

Appendix B, Remarks by Mr. Frederick Catherwood, C.E., On Drainage, British Guiana.

Appendix C, Remarks by Mr. Frederick Catherwood, C.E., On the Substitution of Central Factories for the Present System of Manufacturing Sugar, Dated, 30 October, 1846.

4. Dalton, Henry, *The History of British Guiana*, 2 vols., London, 1867, vol. 1, p. 499.

5. Bayley, Sydney H., *Railways in British Guiana*, op. cit., pp. 14-25, no date.

6. Catherwood, Stephens' *Incidents of Travel in Central America*, op. cit., preface, p. vi.

7. Weber, Shirley W., editor and translator, *Schliemann's First Visit to America 1850-1851*, Cambridge, 1942.

8. Scoles, J. J., *Dictionary of Architecture*, op. cit.

9. Aspinwall-Robinson Correspondence, Collections of the Henry Huntington Library, San Marino, California.

10. Marysville-Benecia Railroad (Newspaper references):

Proposed Railroad from Marysville to Benecia.
Alta California, 29 September, 1852, p. 2, col. 2.
Survey; brief mention.
Sacramento Union, 26 Nov., 1852, p. 2, col. 1.
List of members of survey party.
Sacramento Union, 30 Nov., 1852, p. 2, col. 2.
Survey commenced.
Alta California, 15 Dec., 1852, p. 2, col. 4.
Preliminary survey completed.
Alta California, 14 March, 1853, p. 2, col. 3.
Estimated cost.
Alta California, 12 Feb., 1854, p. 2, col. 3.
Proposed change of terminal from Benecia to Straits of Carquines.
California Chronicle, 4 April, 1856, p. 2, col. 2.
Survey to connect Vallejo with Benecia-Marysville Railroad.
California Chronicle, 26 May, 1856, p. 1, col. 1.
Money subscribed for Marysville-Benecia Railroad.
Alta California, 28 Sept., 1857, p. 2, col. 2.

Marysville-San Francisco Railroad Company organized to further Marysville-Benecia Railroad.
  San Francisco Bulletin, 16 Oct., 1857, p. 2, col. 1.
Directors of Marysville-Benecia to Sacramento to unite with Central Pacific, and continue on to Marysville.
  Sacramento Union, 19 Jan. 1865, p. 2, col. 2.

The survey of the Benecia and Marysville Railroad was completed in March 1853. An election was called by the Council for 28 February, 1854, on the question of a subscription of $800,000 for the Marysville and Benecia National Railroad Company. The result was 953 in favor, and 36 against. On 4 March the amount was subscribed. Benecia promised $250,000. This project was allowed to drop until 1857, when another survey was made. The counties to be traversed by the road, subscribed; Yuba voted to give $200,000, but actually gave bonds for $100,000. The company was organized in October 1857, with a capital of $3,000,000. The road was projected to run to Vallejo, and there connect with boats for San Francisco. In August 1858, a contract was entered into with D. C. Haskin to construct the road bed, lay the track and place the road in running order, with all the necessary buildings, etc.; the price fixed at $3,500,000. In February 1869, a few months before the completion of the Central Pacific, this road was finished to Sacramento. When the former commenced operations a lively opposition sprang up. Great efforts were made to build up Vallejo, and make it the central distributing and receiving city of the State. During the year, 1871, the company, having completed its branch road to Marysville, annexed the Napa Valley and other roads. They also acquired the vessels of the California Steam Navigation Company, and had almost a monopoly of the inland trade. It was at about that time a company was organized by the wealthy owners of the California Pacific road, to construct a railroad from the northern part of Sacramento valley to Ogden, to compete with the Central Pacific. These brilliant plans were foiled by the owners of the overland road buying the majority of shares in the California Pacific, and thereby gaining control. The location of the track proved faulty from Knight's Landing to Marysville through the tule lands. If the line had been run from Knight's Landing east to the bank of Feather River, and then along this higher land to Yuba City, the road would be in running order and successfully operating today. Knight's Landing, on the Sacramento River, is now the terminal point. In the winter of 1871-2, the flood destroyed the bridge, track and trestles across the tule. The road might have been rebuilt had not communication with lower cities been gained by the construction of the California and Oregon Railroad.

Chamberlain, W. H., *History of Yuba County, California*, San Francisco, 1879, p. 111.
Ellis, William T.,
  Memories: My Seventy-two Years in the Romantic County of Yuba, California, The University of Oregon, 1939, pp. 39-40.

Underhill, Reuben L.,
   From Cowhides to Golden Fleece, Palo Alto, 1939.
   (About Thomas O. Larkin and his part in the Benecia-Marysville Railway.)

CHAPTER ELEVEN

1. There are only cryptic records of his last two years in London and these from notes to J. J. Scoles, who wrote his short biography in *The Dictionary of Architecture*. All these notes are from 21 Charles Square, Hoxton, dated between 7 June and 12 June 1852 and concern California.

'21 Charles Square
June 7, 1852

My Dear Scoles

   How are you off for room at the Institute Museum [of Architecture]? and would you like to have a slab of Quartz from California. I mean the Gold bearing kind.

   It is not exactly a building stone although *we use it* for that purpose at the mines.

   I have a rather fine slab which is quite at the service of the Institute if you think it would be acceptable.'

   And another note, dated 9 June, also to Scoles:

'I will have the slab ready by Saturday.

   I should like much to pay you a visit, but the distance and intricacy of the route deter me. However by means of the River and your Map the journey doubtless may be accomplished.

   I am going soon to California but that appears a trifling undertaking to finding out Hammersmith, which to me as an Eastern man seems to be in the far far west.

Ever yours truly
F. Catherwood.

2. References to the Sinking of the *SS Arctic:*
   The New York Times, 13 October 1854, et seq.
   New-York Tribune, 16 October 1854, et seq.
   Illustrated London News, 28 October 1854, p. 415.
   Annual Register 1854, 'Sinking of *SS Arctic*,' pp. 161-3.
   Harper's Monthly Magazine, Editor's Easy Chair, Nov.-Dec. 1854, 'The Loss of the *Arctic*.'
   Monthly Nautical Magazine, vol. 1, p. 105-11, 1854.

   Dow, John G., *The Collins Line*, New York, 1937.

Parker & Bowen, *Mail and Passenger Steamships*, New York, 1927, pp. 15-16.

Reisenberg, Capt. Felix, *Early Steamships*—Currier & Ives Prints, no. 4. The Studio, 1933, page 6, and plate vii.

Tyler, D. B., *Steam Conquers the Atlantic*, ch. xiv, New York, 1927.

BIBLIOGRAPHY OF FREDERICK CATHERWOOD

Views of Ancient Monuments in Central America, Chiapas, and Yucatán, London and New York, 1844.

'Account of the Punico-Libyan Monument at Dugga and the Remains of an Ancient Structure at Bless, near the Site of Ancient Carthage,' *Transactions of the American Ethnological Society*, New York, 1845, vol. i, pp. 477-91; 7 figures in text.

Incidents of Travel in Central America, edited by F. Catherwood, Arthur Hall, Virtue & Co., London, 1854.

With Robert Burford:

Description of a View of the City of Jerusalem. . . Painted from Drawings . . . by F. Catherwood, London, 1835.

Description of a View of the Ruins of the Temple of Baalbec. . . Painted . . . from Drawings . . . by F. Catherwood, London, 1844.

Description of a View of the Great Temple of Karnak and the Surrounding City of Thebes. . . Painted by R. Burford from Drawings by Mr. F. Catherwood, London, 1839.

GENERAL BIBLIOGRAPHY

Alomia, Gustavo Martinez, *Historiadores de Yucatán*, Merida, 1906.

American Art-Union Transactions, New York, 1848.

Anderson, William J., *The Architecture of Ancient Rome*, London, 1947.

Arundale, Francis, *Illustrations of Jerusalem and Mount Sinai, Including the Most Interesting Sites between Grand Cairo and Beyrout*, London, 1837.

Bapst, G., *Essai sur l'histoire des panoramas et des dioramas*, Paris, 1891.

Beattie, William, *Brief Memoir of the Late William Henry Bartlett*, London, 1855.

Belzoni, Giovanni, *Narrative of Operations and Recent Discoveries*, London, 1821.

Besant, Sir Walter, *London in the Eighteenth Century*, London, 1902; *London, North of the Thames*, London, 1911.

Binyon, Laurence, *English Water Colours*, London, 1933.

Birkenhead, Shelia, *Against Oblivion: the Life of Joseph Severn*, London, New York, 1944.

Birnstingl, H. J., *Sir John Soane*, London, 1925.

Black, George F., *The Surnames of Scotland*, New York, 1946.

Blom, Frans, *The Conquest of Yucatán*, Boston, 1936.

Blom, Frans, and LaFarge, Oliver, *Tribes and Temples*, 2 vols., New Orleans, 1926-7.

Blomfield, Reginald, *Architectural Drawings and Draughtsmen*, London, 1912.

Blunden, Edmund, *Leigh Hunt and His Circle*, New York, 1930.

Boulton, Wm. B., *London Amusements*, London, 1901.

Britton, John, *Autobiography*, 2 vols., London, 1850.

Brooks, Van Wyck, *The World of Washington Irving*, New York, 1944.

Brown, Frank P., *London Buildings, Painting and Sculpture*, London, 1933.

Cahill, Holger, *American Sources of Modern Art*, New York, 1933.

Casteñeda, Lenoir, Warden, Fracy, and St. Priest, *Antiquités mexicaines*, Paris, 1834.

Charnay, Desiré, *The Ancient Cities of the New World*, New York, 1887.

Clark, Kenneth, *The Gothic Revival*, London, 1928.

Coghlan, Francis, *The Cicerone or Fashionable Guide to all Places of Amusements*, London, 1830.

Cummings, T. A., *Annals of the National Academy of Design*, New York, 1865.

Dalton, Henry G., *The History of British Guiana*, 2 vols., London, 1855.

Dame, Lawrence, *Yucatán*, New York, 1941.

Dictionary of Architecture, The, 3 vols., London, 1852-93.

Dunlap, William, *History of the Rise and Progress of the Art of Design*, New York, 1865.

Durbin, J. P., *Observations in the East*, 1845.

Duyckinck, Evert Augustus, *Cyclopaedia of American Literature*, 2 vols., New York, 1877.

Early Victorian England, various authors, 2 vols., London, 1934.

Eaton, Sir Frederick, *The Royal Academy and Its Members*, London, 1884.

Ebers, Georg, *Richard Lepsius*, New York, 1897.

Elliott-Joyce, L. E., *Central America*, New York, 1925.

Faure, Elie, *History of Art*, 5 vols., New York, 1921.

Fergusson, James, *History of Architecture in All Countries*, 2 vols., London, 1874.

Finden, William, *Landscape Illustrations of the Bible*, 2 vols., London, 1836.

Fox, Henry Edward, *Journal*, edited by the Earl of Ilchester, London, 1923.

Gann, Thomas, *Maya Cities*, London, 1927.

Gilder, Rodman, *The Battery*, Boston, 1936.

Glueck, Nelson, *The River Jordan*, Philadelphia, 1946.

Gotch, J. A., *The Growth and Work of the Royal Institute of British Architects*, 1834-1934, London, 1934.

Graves, Algernon, *The Royal Academy of Arts: A Complete Dictionary of Contributors and Their Work from Its Foundation in 1769 to 1904*, 8 vols., London, 1905-6.

Hagen, Victor Wolfgang von, *Jungle in the Clouds*, London, 1940; *The Aztec and Maya Papermakers*, New York, 1943; 'F. Catherwood, Arch^t,' *Bulletin of the New-York Historical Society*, January 1946; 'How the Lost Cities of the Mayas Were Rediscovered,' *Travel Magazine*, April 1946; 'Mr. Catherwood Also Is Missing,' *Natural History Magazine*, March 1947; 'Mr. Catherwood's Panorama,' *Magazine of Art*, April 1947; *Maya Explorer, John Lloyd Stephens and the Lost Cities of Central America and Yucatán*, Norman, Okla., 1947.

Halle, Louis J., Jr., *River of Ruins*, New York, 1941.

Halls, J. J., *Life and Correspondence of Henry Salt*, 2 vols., London, 1834.

Hamlin, Talbot, *Architecture through the Ages*, New York, 1940.

Harncourt, Rene d', and Douglas, Frederic H., *Indian Art of the United States*, New York, 1941.

Haslip, Joan, *Lady Hester Stanhope*, London, 1934.

Hay, Robert, *Illustrations of Cairo*, lithographed by John C. Bourne, London, 1840.

Hilmy, Ibrahim, *The Literature of Egypt and the Soudan from the Earliest Times to the Year 1885 Inclusive: A Bibliography*, London, 1886.

Hollingshead, John, *The Story of Leicester Square*, London, 1892; *My Life Time*, London, 1895.

Holmes, W. H., *Archaeological Studies among the Ancient Cities of Mexico*, Chicago, 1895.

Hoskins, George Alexander, *A Visit to the Great Oasis of the Libyan Desert*, London, 1837.

Humboldt, Alexander von, *Vues de Cordillerès*, Paris, 1810.

Hussey, Christopher, *The Picturesque*, New York, 1927.

Huxley, Aldous, *Beyond the Mexique Bay*, New York, 1934.

Joyce, T. A., *Maya and Mexican Art*, London, no date.

Kelemen, Pál, *Medieval American Art*, 2 vols., New York, 1943; *Battlefield of the Gods*, London, 1936.

Lane-Poole, Stanley, *Life of Edward William Lane*, London, 1877.

Lewis, Wilmarth Sheldon, *Three Tours through London*, New Haven, 1944.

Los Mayas Antiguos, various authors, Mexico, 1941.

Lothrop, Samuel K., *Tulum: An Archaeological Study of the East Coast of Yucatán,* Washington, 1924.

Lowell, Amy, *John Keats,* 2 vols., Boston, 1925.

Ludwig, Emil, *Schliemann,* Boston, 1931.

Magoffin, R. H. D., and Davis, Emily, *Magic Spades,* New York, 1929.

Maudslay, Alfred P., *A Glimpse of Guatemala,* London, 1899.

The Maya and Their Neighbors, various authors, New York, 1940.

Means, Philip A., *Newport Tower,* New York, 1942.

Michaelis, A., *A Century of Archaeological Discoveries,* New York, 1908.

Mitchell, Leslie J., *The Conquest of the Maya,* New York, 1935.

Morley, S. G., *The Inscriptions at Copán,* Washington, 1920; *The Ancient Maya,* Palo Alto, 1946.

Mumford, Lewis, *The Culture of Cities,* New York, 1941.

Newberry, Percy C., 'Topographical Notes on Western Thebes,' *Annales du service des antiquities de l'Egypte,* Paris, 1906, tome VII.

Odell, George, *Annals of the New York Stage,* 2 vols., New York, 1862.

Peel, Mrs. C. S., *The Stream of Time,* New York, 1932.

Phelps-Stokes, I. N., *The Iconography of Manhattan Island,* 1498-1909, 5 vols., New York, 1922-6.

Porter, Bertha, and Moss, Rosalind, *Topographical Bibliography of Ancient Egyptian Hieroglyphic Texts, Reliefs and Pai Paintings,* 2 vols., Oxford, 1929.

Praz, Mario, *The Romantic Agony,* New York, 1930.

Prescott, William H., *The Conquest of Mexico,* New York, 1843.

Quennell, Peter, *Byron in Italy,* New York, 1941.

Redgrave, Samuel, *A Dictionary of Artists of the English School,* London, 1878.

Rees, Thomas, *Reminiscences of Literary London,* 1799-1853, London, 1896.

Robinson, Alfred, *Life in California,* New York, 1846.

Roget, John Lewis, *History of the Old Water Colour Society,* London, 1891.

Rollins, Hyder E., *The Keats Circle . . .* (1806-1878), 2 vols., Cambridge, 1948.

Sabin, Joseph, *Bibliotheca Americana,* 29 vols., New York, 1868-1937.

Sadleir, Michael, *The Strange Life of Lady Blessington,* London, 1933.

Sandby, William, *History of the Royal Academy,* London, 1862.

Saville, Marshall, *Bibliographic Notes on Uxmal,* New York, 1921; *Bibliographic Notes on Palenque,* New York, 1928.

Schliemann, Heinrich, *Schliemann's First Visit to America,* 1850-51, edited and translated by Shirley W. Weber, Cambridge, 1942.

168

Sharp, William, *Life and Letters of Joseph Severn*, London, 1878.

Sitwell, Sacheverell, *British Architects and Craftsmen*, London, 1945.

Spinden, Herbert J., *A Study of Maya Art*, Cambridge, 1913.

Spittlefields and Shoreditch in an uproar or, to devil to pay with the English and Irish, London, 1736.

Stephens, John Lloyd, *Incidents of Travel in Central America, Chiapas, and Yucatán*, 2 vols., New York, 1841; *Incidents of Travel in Yucatan*, 2 vols., New York, 1843.

Tallis, John, *London Street Views*, London, 1839.

Taylor, Tom, *Leicester Square, Its Association and Its Worthies*, London, 1874.

Thieme-Becker, *Allgemeines Lexikon der Bildenden Kunstler*, Leipzig, 1907.

Trevelyan, George M., *British History in the 19th Century*, London, 1923.

Tyler, David B., *Steam Conquers the Atlantic*, New York, 1927.

Underhill, Reuben L., *From Cowhides to Golden Fleece*, Palo Alto, 1939.

Waldeck, Frederic de, *Voyage pittoresque et archéologique*, Paris, 1838.

—— and Brasseur de Bourbourg, C. E., *Recherches sur les ruines de Palenqué*, Paris, 1866.

Whitley, William T., *Art in England* 1800-1820, London, 1927.

Wilkinson, Sir John G., *Thebes and Egypt*, London, 1835.

Wilson, James Grant, *The Memorial History of the City of New York*, 4 vols., New York, 1893.

Winwar, Francis, *The Romantic Rebels*, New York, 1935.

Wood and Dakins, *Baalbec*, London, 1757.